Arthur Griffiths

The Queen's Shilling

Vol. 1

Arthur Griffiths

The Queen's Shilling
Vol. 1

ISBN/EAN: 9783337307608

Printed in Europe, USA, Canada, Australia, Japan

Cover: Foto ©Thomas Meinert / pixelio.de

More available books at **www.hansebooks.com**

THE QUEEN'S SHILLING.

A SOLDIER'S STORY.

BY

CAPTAIN ARTHUR GRIFFITHS,

Author of "Peccavi; or, Geoffrey Singleton's Mistake."

VOL. I.

LONDON:
HENRY S. KING & CO., 65, CORNHILL.

1872.

CONTENTS.

VOL. I.

CHAPTER I.
PAGE

SCAGGLETON 1

CHAPTER II.
ALURED FRERE TAKES THE SHILLING 13

CHAPTER III.
IN LONDON 33

CHAPTER IV.
STARTING 49

CHAPTER V.
FAIRLY OFF 70

CHAPTER VI.
"THE CUSTOM OF WAR IN LIKE CASES" . . . 93

CHAPTER VII.
LIFE AT THE DEPOT 113

CONTENTS.

CHAPTER VIII.
                                                    PAGE
MOYNEHAN CASTLE: ON THE THRESHOLD . . . 128

CHAPTER IX.
MOYNEHAN CASTLE: GAINING GROUND . . . 148

CHAPTER X.
MOYNEHAN CASTLE: QUITE AT HOME . . . 164

CHAPTER XI.
THE ROUTE 181

CHAPTER XII.
THE VOYAGE OUT 196

CHAPTER XIII.
AT THE FRONT 210

CHAPTER XIV.
BATTLE AND SIEGE 227

CHAPTER XV.
A CHANCE SHOT 246

The Queen's Shilling.

———o———

CHAPTER I.—(*Prologue.*)

SCAGGLETON CASTLE.

> "Hast thou seen that lordly castle,
> That castle by the sea?
> Golden and red above it,
> The clouds float gorgeously."
> LONGFELLOW'S *Translation of Uhland.*

ON the east coast, somewhere between Norfolk and Northumberland, there stands an ancient but decayed fishing-village, named Scaggleton. The place had been of importance once, probably in the time of the Danes, when Olaf the Burly built the stronghold whose ruins stand to this day on St. Bungo's Hill, and the rovers piled up a cairn of stones on Scatheness Spit to guide themselves in and out. But since that time Scaggleton had gone down in the world, and the fault lay with the German Ocean. The sea played such tricks with the land,—here encroaching, there receding; making its daily dinner off the *débris* of St. Olaf's Castle, vomiting forth the same at the far end of the Bay; filling up the harbour with mud at one place, at another retreating altogether, and leaving great, bald, bare banks of shingle, or dreary reaches of waste sand high and dry, far above the topmost tide-mark—that the Scaggleton people gave up the fight. They succumbed to the sea, and became its vassals: amphibious salt water bipeds, without a thought beyond their nets, and the herring season, and their clumsy fishing boats with tan-dried sails.

The town itself lay in the northern angle of the wide shallow bay, gathered up into a bunch at the foot of some crags, where the river Scaggle struggled sluggishly and painfully through choking sand-heaps to the sea. On all sides but this one, the landscape displayed nothing but long, rolling billows of down-land, covered with long rank grass, and fringed with a belt of sand and shingle. Here and there upon the beach was a lugger run up high and dry, or a handful of boats, or a group of small children who had wandered away from the town to poke among the holes for crabs. Beyond these, nothing broke the monotony of the expanse save the white, dusty, lonely high-road that came from Coxmouth and went by Scaggleton to Coxmolton. By—not through; for the queen's highway despised Scaggleton and its fish-scales, and disdaining to cross the antique drawbridge, which was the sole gate to the town, turned off to the right upon the southern side of the Scaggle.

Scaggleton owned just three streets, radiating all of them from a common centre—the market-place. One led to the drawbridge; a second, degenerating into a lane, joined by-and-by the high-road farther up the stream; and the third was the approach to Scaggleton Crags and Castle.

To hear it mentioned simply—Scaggleton Castle—sounds rather big. But although it was the seat of Christopher Norreys, Esquire, it was only a "bogus" castle after all. This Mr. Norreys who owned it, had built it thinking to cheat himself and all the world into believing that he had inherited it from his ancestors.

Mr. Norreys was a cadet of a noble family; a man who had married early in life a woman as poor as himself. Children had come tumbling into the world with such indecent haste, that food became scarce in the Norreys' household. Relatives, in high place, after much importuning, lent a helping hand, and tried to do something for their poor cousin. He was appointed first Her Majesty's Consul at the Azimbogee River; then Receiver-general at Honduras; later he became a magistrate on the frontier of Caffraria; and then Secretary to the Colonial Government of a West India island. He drifted from one place to another, finding something unsuitable in each, and at last, like a species of social flotsam and jetsam, whom no one cared to own, he found himself stranded in England. Just then his wife inherited a few thousand pounds, and died almost immediately—probably of the good news. The grief of this bereavement nearly broke Mr. Norreys down. He sought high and low for a place to dwell in, and by chance he stumbled upon Scaggleton. It was so desolate and retired, that it seemed of all places the one to suit him. Hither he brought his little ones, and built them a home. If anything had been needed to prove him of unsound mind, this house of his would have supplied the missing link. It was in itself the strongest evidence against him.

At a distance, Scaggleton Castle looked as old as the ruins of St. Bungo's Hill. Inspected closely, it was an undeniable sham. Lying in a little *cul-de-sac* of a bay, just round the corner beyond Scaggleton, you might have thought at first sight of its turrets and battlements, its portcullis and loopholed walls, that you had come upon an old fashioned fortified stronghold of the middle ages. Yet from first to last Scaggleton Castle was a delusion and a snare; artificial and pretentious throughout; about as real as the rock-work of an open air theatre at Rosherville or Cremorne. In front of the house ran a narrow strip of garden where nothing grew, and a few yards of drive coming up from the gate, guarded by a gingerbread portcullis. The worm-eaten gate and the rickety towers that did duty for a lodge would have sought as vainly to shut out intruders, as the rough sea-wall which fenced in the garden succeeded in keeping the boisterous waves at bay. A mock bastion or two bulged out from this barrier-wall, and all along it were painted sham portholes, in black circles upon a line of whitewash. Such was the external aspect of Scaggleton Castle. Inside, low rooms, dark and gloomy, narrow passages, and spiral staircases, were the penalty exacted for the picturesqueness of its mediæval architecture.

But those who sneered at the Castle must perforce have praised its natural surroundings. What man had built might be a hollow mockery; there was no such fault to be found with nature's handiwork round Scaggleton Castle. The rugged old cliff, beneath which the house crouched, yearning as it were for sympathy, was itself no sham; nor were the broad patches of gorse that brightened here and there the green sloping bank above; still less the rocks that lay heaped up in variegated stacks, purple, grey, blue, black, and brown, at the base of the sea wall. There was no make-believe about the rich masses of tangled sea-weed, or the glistening pools, or the grand old sea that was so changeful in all its moods. One day you might have tickled the old villain with a straw as he lay, so smooth and peaceable and quiet; the next day he came tumbling in over the rocks, deluging the house, and wetting the very cliff behind with spray. Oh, how dreary then was that solitary house over above the beach! How the wind beat straight in upon its panes of glass and whistled through the sashes! playing now a shrill solo with long-drawn mournful notes, now gathering up all the strength of its wild orchestra—roaring waves and raindrops rattling like drum taps—and making such a clatter that it shook this pasteboard castle from roof-tree to cellar. See! the waves enlisted to serve in earnest, press forward and will not be denied. They may draw back, but it is only to gain fresh strength. Sweeping out, not discomfited, but as a *ruse de guerre;* re-forming in sullen steadfastness their long battle lines of billows, till, recruited and reinforced, they gather courage to charge forward again with increasing pace and louder thunder, amid the boom as of great guns, and the flashing of foam-flakes like rapid musketry, as if bent upon carrying all by storm.

It was here that six motherless girls had been left to grow up as best they could. Their father never troubled his head about them. I do not believe he knew them all by name. There were so many, how was he to distinguish one from the other? Margaretta was monstrous like Millicent, and Mary was like them both; he confused Agatha with Beatrice; and Patience, the youngest born, got between his legs, and was too small to be seen. Mr. Norreys, after his wife's death, and their settlement at Scaggleton, lived on, a hopelessly dull grey, almost colourless, sort of existence, exercising no supervision over his children, vainly seeking to stifle grief by violent exercise—walking the country through, touching the porch of every church before he returned home, serving as a volunteer in the Life Boat, spending nights at sea with the Scaggleton fishermen.

The responsibility which he refused was assumed to some extent by the elder girls, but all alike, had much their own way. They were a madcap crew leading a savage, open-air sort of existence, that gave a hue of health to their tanned cheeks, and an active grace to their well formed lissome figures. It would take a book to describe the games at which they played. Tom-boys, all of them, addicted from earliest childhood to all sorts of climbing feats, venturesome walking along planks or on the extreme edge of the sea-wall when the tide was high enough to drown them; pretending one day to be Red Indians on the war-path with berry-stained faces, the next to be a handful of ship-wrecked mariners, gathered forlorn around the fire they had lighted in some rocky crevice; fishing, gardening, building, uprooting, they were always in mischief, always all over the place, screaming with laughter, and shaking out their manes of bright tufted hair at each new joke and gesture. After all, Scaggleton Castle was their own place—their own special domain. The small quiet bay, hemming in their mock fortress as with a private moat, was all their own, where they were at liberty to paddle about unmolested all day long, knee-deep in the crystal water, as they hunted for sea anemones and curious marine treasures. So, too, the rocky cliff behind the house was home park and playground, owning a dozen shallow chasms and unmysterious caves, every inch of which they knew by heart, and had drawn from end to end in search of wild flowers and sea plants and rubbish.

Their early training, as might have been expected, bore fruit as they grew up to womanhood. They became one and all singularly free-spoken, merry-hearted, natural girls. The constant exposure and the vigorous exercise of their daily life developed a blooming healthiness that was quite pleasant to look upon. You might have searched the whole country through before you met a bevy of brighter, prettier creatures. And they were as unconventional in thought and action as they were elastic of step and pure in their young inexperienced hearts. It was a pity they could not be left to live on as they had grown up from infancy, uncontaminated by the world and its ways. It needed no sage to predict that these warm-hearted impulsive young women would awake some day to the realities of life, to learn by experience that stronger feelings existed in the human heart than the love, however deep and passionate, of sister towards sister.

Beyond their family circle, the Norreys saw no one at Scaggleton Castle. The county people had found their overtures of kindness rejected from the first; and in the town of Scaggleton itself, there was no society whatever. It was quite by accident that Sir Herbert Hunnisett came across them.

This great personage was owner of the yacht *Zobeide*, which, as he said himself, had been driven into Scaggleton by stress of weather. The baronet (he took care to proclaim his name and title) told them this, and a good deal more, the day he called at the Castle and introduced himself. "Was *en route* with his yacht to Norway. Always went to Norway for the fishing. Sometimes to the moors though. But the season in town had been very trying. He was glad to get away." There was something in the man's manner which Mr. Norreys did not like. The metal had not quite a true ring; the man was too glib and off-hand. But with the girls he was quite divine. Can you not understand it, reader? It was the first man (Norreys *père* excepted) who had ever darkened the Castle doors. And Sir Herbert was such a jaunty, devil-may-care, smartly-dressed man. He exhibited such flashing rings, such chain-cable watch-guards, and swaggered so gracefully in his blue yachting-suit, that the girls could not resist him. They were young and impressionable, inexperienced, and had already begun to find Scaggleton "slow." For some weeks Sir Herbert was perpetually in and out of the house. The old gentleman fed him and made him welcome; the young ladies petted him, and listened with rapt attention to his tales of the grand world of London.

His intimacy with the family did not end here. He evinced his gratitude to Mr. Norreys by eloping with the eldest daughter.

Grief and shame took possession of that quiet household—woe to be intensified a thousand-fold by the discovery that Sir Herbert was an impostor. The yacht belonged to his master, whose groom the villain was.

CHAPTER II.

ALURED FRERE TAKES THE SHILLING.

> "For gold the merchant ploughs the main,
> The farmer ploughs the manor;
> But glory is the sodger's prize,
> The sodger's wealth is honour."
>
> BURNS.

IT was the winter of '54—the most cheerless period of that dread season when Crimean affairs were at their worst. Gloom hung over every English home. Vacant chairs that must remain empty for evermore stood by many an English hearth that Christmas-tide. Terrible tales of carnage, of famine, of pestilence, of woes unutterable, came from that far-off land where, upon the thirsty soil, English blood was poured out like water. Many an English mother spent nights in agonized prayer for the safety of her dearest child; wives wailed for absent husbands who were standing in the forefront of danger; all alike shared the common suspense, dreading from hour to hour the possible tidings of grief and sorrow. Nature, as if in deference to the agony of the nations, draped herself in her wintry pall. The dull leaden sky was hung with mournful weeds, and as evening closed in, the bitter snow-blast howled piteous dirges across the desert places, or sighed melancholy requiems amongst the branches of the bare leafless trees.

It was barely five o'clock in the evening; but the lights were burning brightly, and the members of Major Frere's family were seated round the fire in the drawing-room of Scaggleton Castle. Ten years have passed since the events recorded in the first chapter, and Scaggleton is now in other hands. Mr. Norreys succeeding most unexpectedly to the family honours left, nothing loth, a place grown thoroughly hateful since his daughter's disappearance. Major Frere had bought the Castle, because it promised to house his large family comfortably. Moreover, Coxmouth College was close at hand, where his sons were at school. Scaggleton was little changed. It had assumed, perhaps, a more habitable look, thanks to the mistress it now owned.

Mrs. Frere, a shrewd woman of the world, who had shared with her husband the ups and downs of a long military service, was able to make a better show than poor thriftless Norreys. But although more snug within than of old, without the scene was as wild as ever. It seemed this night a light-house, an Eddystone, a mansion cradled among the howling winds, beaten by the crashing breakers of an angry sea.

There were four persons present: the owner of Scaggleton, Robert Frere, a retired officer; his wife, a graceful stately woman, past her first youth; and their two daughters, Dorothy and Lilian. All were dressed in the deepest mourning. But without this it was easy to perceive, from the hushed, subdued air of the whole party, that they were in the presence of, or had lately passed through, some crushing grief. The mother sat idly gazing into the deep mysterious glow of the burning coals; the major pretended to read, but he got up every moment to poke the fire nervously, or draw back the heavy curtains to look out on the dark forbidding night; the girls were at work, and spoke their little nothings almost in whispers. Dorothy, now the eldest of the family, was a beauty, with a sober, quiet face; long lashes veiled her meek eyes, and the rich masses of hair were kept close to the soft cheek in unpretending plaits.

Lilian's was a different style of loveliness. Impetuous life mantled beneath the clear olive skin, sending in a second crimson flashes to her face. They were a handsome family, one and all.

For the fiftieth time Major Frere fidgets with the fire-irons, taking up poker and tongs in turn, and throwing them down with a bang upon the grate. For the fiftieth time he undoes the fastening of the shutters, and looks out.

"How late he is!" at last comes out, almost with a growl.

"The coach is hardly due at Scaggleton yet, father," remarks Dorothy, pointing to the clock.

"I daresay he will walk. It's barely ten miles," Lilian says.

"I'm sure I hope he won't. He's not half strong, and if the cold were to get into his chest——"

"Why, mother, Alured is as strong as a horse!" is Dorothy's answer.

"Mother and her dear boys!" Lilian cried, forgetting for the instant the sorrow that weighed them down. The words were not past her lips before she could have bitten her tongue through and through for her thoughtlessness.

"Oh! forgive me, mother—I—" then the impulsive child's eyes filled with tears, and there was a dead silence.

Boys! There was no longer a plural for the word in that house. The tale might be read in those black weeds that clothed them all. Death in the guise of a Russian bullet had met Robert Frere, the eldest son, at Inkerman. The sad news was but a week or two old.

Alured Frere, the only surviving son, was expected that night from school, from Coxmouth College, where Robert, who was now no more, had also received his education.

The time slipped by gradually. At length an uproar in the hall announced the arrival of the light-hearted schoolboy. In a second the drawing-room was thrown open, and the whole party, mother excepted, rushed out to meet—

" Alured !"

" Old boy !"

" Back safe and sound at last. What on earth made you so late, sir ?"

Such were the greetings from his father and his sisters.

"And mother ?" Alured asked, pushing on at once into the room, because he guessed why she had not come out too to kiss him. Her grief at the loss of that other, over whose distant nameless grave the earth had hardly hardened yet, was far too fresh to make it otherwise than painful to meet the younger son.

" She is here, darling," cried the mother, clasping him in her arms. You are all that is left to me now, my boy ; my boy !"

"I will try my best, mother. But I know I can never be like Robert to you."

" You're a good boy, Alured !" she replied, fondly stroking his light curly locks.

There was a pause as mother and son

stood hand locked in hand : she with heart overflowing with memories of the irrevocable past; he with mind resolved to do his best to soothe her sorrow. It was the soft-hearted thoughtful woman who first recovered herself.

"But you are wet, my darling : go and change at once."

"How did you come ? The coach was due long ago."

"I walked, on my ten toes."

"What! walk in such weather as this?" exclaimed Mrs. Frere. "Do go and change."

"Why, I'm not made of salt."

"Or of sugar," said Lilian, laughing.

"Already ? I owe you one."

"Don't stop chattering and scuffling," interposed the Major. "Go along with you, Alured. Be off."

Half-an-hour afterwards, they were seated round the dinner-table, at a sociable sort of tea-dinner meal. Suddenly, the heavy sullen-toned bell, a legacy from Mr. Norreys, of the outer gate sounded through the house.

"At this time of night ? Who can it be."

"The postman."

"Psha! the postman ought to have come hours ago."

"Old Filey don't trouble himself to come out, that's what it is," said Dorothy. "When it's a bad night, he waits till the morning."

Further discussion was ended by the entrance of Isabella, the maid, with a handful of letters. The advent of the postman was by no means a matter of joy to the Frere family. It was he who had brought them the list of the killed and wounded. How vividly was that miserable night remembered! In these days of telegraphs victories precede, after them come the butcher's bills. The gladness of the first is soon deadened by the details that follow.

"There's a long letter for papa," said Lilian, pointing.

"How can you tell whether it's long or short, until its opened, stupid?"

"I mean long in length, Alured—not in breadth."

"You don't know what you mean, miss. Don't let it occur again."

Lillian made a face at him, as if to show she didn't care twopence.

"It's only an official," said the major, to whom long narrow envelopes inscribed "On Her Majesty's Service" were no novelty. "It will keep I daresay."

"Do open it at once, papa," cried Lilian, "and tell us all about it."

"Patience on a monument——"

"We'll wait till after dinner, I think," said Mrs. Frere, and that ended the matter. Papa was often hasty and sharp in his tones, but a few quiet words from mamma met with a much more prompt obedience.

Father and son were alone when the wonderful letter was unsealed, and the lad was able to scan unobserved the elder man's face, as with clouded brow the major perused its contents.

It was dated Horse Guards, December 1854, and ran as follows :—

"SIR,—I have it in command to convey to you the gracious pleasure of Her Majesty the Queen, that the vacancy caused by the death of your son, Ensign Frere, 145th, killed in action, should be offered for the acceptance of your son, Mr. Alured Frere, whose name is already entered upon the Commander-in-Chief's list. Should it meet your views to accept this commission for your son, I am to request you will inform me when Mr. Frere will be prepared to undergo the examination at Sandhurst.

"I have," etc.

"Well, father?"

"There is nothing in this letter, my boy, that I can tell you of; at least for the present."

The Freres had few secrets among them, and Alured had the good sense to understand that the contents of this letter were not to be discussed.

But later that night, when the family had separated, leaving husband and wife alone, Major Frere communicated to her the substance of the Military Secretary's letter. He did so in fear and trembling, for the death of the eldest son was so recent a grief, that to speak of Alured's departure along the same road—was to reopen the sore; and when Mrs. Frere had read the letter through, she looked at her husband with such a yearning gaze that the Major was filled with compunction at having thrust this fresh sorrow on his wife. Better to have refused spontaneously the profferred offer than have subjected a tender mother's heart to a thousand additional pangs.

"Surely, Robert, you do not ask me to let him go too? I cannot suffer it. I cannot indeed. Not both my boys. I cannot give them both. Was not one enough? What mother has done more? Robert's blood is on Her Flag they tell me;"—this eldest son of theirs was carrying the Queen's Colour when he met his death at Inkerman;—"does she want Alured's too? Do not let them send him also to those shambles. Spare him, Robert; spare him and me, for the love of Heaven."

It was more than she could bear.

At this hour when the memory of her slaughtered first-born was still raw and bleeding, to call upon her to resign her second to the same danger, perhaps to the same death, was more than she could endure. With a shudder she dropped her hands from his arm, where they had been convulsively clenched, and resting her head upon them, on the table, burst into a passionate flood of tears.

"I ought not to have asked you this, Alice. I should have decided myself to refuse. I will write at once to Sir Octavius. But it was kindly meant; you must allow that."

"You have not spoken to Alured yet?"

"Not yet, of course. I would not till I knew what you wished."

"Wished; I wish to keep him. I wish never to let him go out of my sight. I wish to be certain that he can never come to harm."

"My dear, let us drop the subject for the present. To-morrow you will be better able to decide."

But next morning Major Frere did not broach the subject to his wife, and no one could have read in this brave woman's calm features the bitterness that was gnawing at her heart. She went through the morning's work quickly and methodically as was her wont. Read prayers, made the tea, ordered dinner, set her youngest daughter a lesson in French, heedless of all entreaties for a holiday on the plea of Alured's return from school. But her household duties done, she sought her husband in the dining-room, which the major used during the forenoon as a study.

"Have you written to Sir Octavius?" she asked.

"Yes; I have drafted a letter, but it cannot go till this evening."

"May I read it?"

"Of course. It is a refusal, worded as civilly as I can put it;" and he gave the rough copy into her hand.

"Robert," said Mrs. Frere, after she had read the letter through slowly, and looking steadfastly into her husband's eyes, "I will be guided by you solely and entirely in this. Do you think he ought to go?"

The major knew full well all that it cost her to concede this much, to keep the mastery over her feelings that were rampant within. But the emotion displayed on the previous night was now invisible. Her face was impassive, almost cold, though inwardly she was torn with the agony of Rachel mourning for her children.

"I think honestly that it is a great opportunity. It will give the lad such an excellent start."

"He is so young, Robert: only sixteen last

month," pleaded the mother—anything for an excuse.

"He is older than I was when I was in the army of occupation in France."

"But the wars were over then."

"I wish they hadn't been. I should have been more than a major now, after all these years of service, if I had had such an opening as Alured is offered in such stirring times."

"You have always said that the army was no profession for a poor man or a poor man's son."

"Nor is it, when it *is* no profession, when there is no business stirring. But when a soldier can work at his trade—the real trade of war—then it is the most glorious career I know."

Major Frere was speaking from his own "platform"; his was the opinion of a soldier, merely, about soldiering.

"You mean we ought to accept this commission?"

"I do, most assuredly."

"Could you not get him into some other regiment,—one not at the war,—in the colonies, or even in India?"

"I will try if you wish, but I cannot hope my request will be granted."

"Try, Robert; try."

"I will. But it would be folly not to accept the commission as frankly as the offer is made."

"I consent to his going, but save him from the war," she cried, breaking down utterly, her eyes streaming with tears, her voice harsh and thick. "If he, too, should fall it would kill me, I think."

"His fate is in the hands of an all-powerful God, Alice. He might fall dead at our feet this very day, here in our peaceful home, where no danger threatens."

"His will be done," said the mother solemnly, and the discussion was at an end.

So Alured Frere accepted the queen's commission, and at the early age of sixteen years and one month he was engaged to lend his powerful aid in the reduction of Sabastopol.

This lad, Alured Frere, is our hero. Let me endeavour to describe him as he was at this time. A child, really, still; quite ignorant of the world and its ways, except so far as they had been revealed to him in the back regions of a second-rate public school. Till now his horizon had been limited indeed. To become the head of his house, or of the school eventually, was his highest ambition; his daily dreams to win the Lord Bishop's prize for Latin elegiacs, to read Aristophanes or Sophocles without a crib, or to have as much money in his pockets as Smithers, the brewer's son. Yet here was he suddenly pitchforked into greatness. Of a truth, some are born great, and some have greatness thrust upon them. The greatness which overtook Alured was of a kind to raise him to a pinnacle far above the clouds of his schoolboy life. There was to be a great gulf fixed now between him and his associates of yesterday. They were to be kept grinding at the mill, and he was to be taken to the field of glory. Head-master and junior master, usher and præpostor, none of these would have terrors for Alured more. He was no longer to be locked up at nightfall, to be forced into hateful tasks, or fed on filthy food. He was like a gay moth, emerging from the chrysalis. Scarlet and gold were to be his gorgeous plumes for the future. He who had never been in London in all his short life, who had never enjoyed the privilege of paying a bill, whose wardrobe did not own a tail-coat, was to become at a stroke of the pen his own master. Free to smoke and drink, and go to the bad. Free to run into debt and to trifle with young affections, and to dress twice a day in gorgeous apparel wherein to parade the streets of a garrison town.

But to be a soldier had been Alured's fondest dream, ever since he could remember. The major, a poor man, had set his face against it, knowing that he could not support two sons in the army. So when Robert was commissioned, Alured was fain to relinquish his hopes, and to content himself with what might offer by-and-by. Not the less did he dream over the career he was not permitted to embrace. Not the less did he con and learn by heart all that appertained to war, to the study of the trade he loved. When still quite a child he had read from end to end books like " Napier's Battles and Sieges," and Cox's " Life of Marlborough;" " The Life and Adventures of John Ship," " Cyril Thornton," and " The Romance of

War," were among his most treasured library books. As a youngster he had played at soldiers, and was always ready to enroll himself as a volunteer in any band of urchins to parade the streets with handkerchiefs as banners and swords of lath. At last, suddenly and unexpectedly, he reached the summit of his hopes. He was to be an officer, a leader of men, at a time when other boys were being birched. It was well for Alured Frere that he had been carefully brought up, or this sudden promotion would have turned his head. But the lad had never wanted ballast. He was not a crank, tall-masted ship, to be thrown on his beam-ends by the first blast of prosperity. It will be found rather, that his premature call to higher functions braced his energies. Instead of upsetting the lad, it steadied him. It aroused him to the reality that he was now at the helm himself, steering his own craft through a dangerous sea. He was only too anxious to show himself worthy of the high fate—it was so to him—that had become his. Those qualities of steadiness, force of character, unswerving attention to duty, and strong self-reliance, which are to a man as his best friend, were still in the germ, waiting to bud and bear fruit in the experience that time alone gives. On the surface he appeared a shy retiring lad, innocent and guileless, with faith unshaken in the world and in his fellow-creatures. He was of pure metal; but the virgin ore is often soft and yielding. It lacks that coarse admixture of alloy, the rough oxidization that exposure gives it, ere it becomes fit material for time, the workman, to hammer and wield it into enduring shapes.

In appearance our hero was slightly above the middle height, slender in figure, but well knit and active. But on first inspection you were not at liberty to notice these details. It was his face that engrossed all your attention; it struck you at once as God's own gift, so wonderfully handsome was it, and withal so intelligent and high-bred. His cheeks were still smooth, but he had plenty of dark brown hair. Eyes, a clear bright blue, as 'yet unconscious of their power; eyes in which a woman might well be contented to see the reflection of her own; eyes yet untrained, like his thoughts, to love. And there was something in his manner quite as winning as in his face: a mixture of manliness and modesty; independence of spirit, tempered with tenderness and consideration for others. He could not fail to do well. A boy like this could never come to harm. Thus hoped his father, and his mother would not have been less sanguine had she been able to assure herself that he was not doomed to die an early death.

How Alured fared in his journey through life it is the object of these pages to recount.

CHAPTER III.

IN LONDON.

"Primeramente, oh hijo, has de temer a Dios; porque en el temerle está la sabiduria, y siendo sabio no podrás errar en nada."—CERVANTES : *Don Quijote.*

First, oh my son, must you fear God ; because in fearing Him is wisdom, and being wise you can never go wrong.

A FEW posts brought back instructions for Alured to present himself at Sandhurst forthwith.

"How about the examination, boy? Can you pass?" asked his father.

Alured was doubtful.

"We had better give you a run for a week or two at some good army coach's."

"And when do you think of starting?" asked Mrs. Frere nervously.

"The sooner the better. To-morrow."

"Oh, Robert!"

Then silence fell upon them all. This was not the first message of the kind that had reached the Freres. Just a year before, the same order had come to Robert, the eldest son. Mrs. Frere bethought herself of the day when the first-born had gone forth in the heyday of life and strength. The adieux then said and the kisses she had pressed on his youthful brow were still fresh in her mind. Now Alured, the second, was *en route* for the same goal. The mother fairly gave way, and the others caught the infection. That night they lived again the night of anguish which had followed the announcement of Inkerman's victory. The girls sobbed themselves to sleep, and Robert Frere sought in vain to solace his wife in her affliction.

Next day after nightfall father and son started for London. The parting was a dismal affair, though Mrs. Frere tried to cheat herself into some comfort by fancying that the final farewell was not to be said just yet. She counted upon seeing Alured again before he set out on his long and perilous journey. Major Frere intended otherwise, but had said nothing out of consideration for his wife's feelings—but cruel kindness after all. He had resolved to launch Alured straight from London, without revisiting Scaggleton even for a day. He felt that he dared not expose her to the sufferings which that final parting must inevitably occasion; sufferings protracted through the days that the Castle would be littered with the paraphernalia of the young soldier's outfit, the box and sword-case, gun and bullock-trunk, the counterpart of last year's preparations. Such things would recall too vividly the past. So when Alured left Scaggleton, he left it for good.

They reached London early on the following morning and were landed after a fatiguing journey at their lodgings in a quiet street off the Strand, leading down to the river, just as the throbbing, high pulsed life of the great city was beating most vigorously. The effect upon Alured, fresh from stagnant Scaggleton and his mother's apron strings, was almost astounding. He had never dreamt that London was like this. The shifting, changing current of people was like the endless rush of rapid waters. The hurrying, excited crowds of human beings, pressing onward, onward; the noise, the din of wheels and of voices, the cries new and strange, sharp and discordant,—all these stunned, dazed, terrified him. He was lifted off his feet as it were; jostled mind and body. Nor was it possible for him to shake himself free from the strange fascination that possessed him even when ensconced in his dingy little bedroom in Northumberland Street. Even here the racket and turmoil followed him. The hubbub outside still rattled in his ears, and the voices seemed to be entreating him with loud and persistent iteration to come out, and join them in the great stream of life.

"A hat you must have, at once," says the Major peremptorily, "before we do anything else."

"I hate hats!"

"Nonsense, Alured! You can't wear anything else in London."

"Then I hate London."

Hate London! Heaven save the mark! Would he always speak thus of the great Babylon with which he was yet barely on terms of ordinary acquaintance? And all for a silly cap he had won at football last term. But his father knew better, and marched the lad at once to a well-known hat-shop in the Strand; then turning westward, and passing into Trafalgar Square, they crossed to Pall Mall, where the elder pointed out the clubs, Union, Athenæum, United Service, and the " Rag."

" What an odd name for a club, papa."

" Yes ; it is. The Rag and Famish they call it in full," said Major Frere laughingly. " We'll get your name put down for it one of these days."

" I think I'd rather belong to one of the others."

" Would you ? Why ? "

" I don't like the name."

Again the major laughed, and was about to explain, when he heard himself called to by name from the top of the wide steps that lead to the portal of this club.

" Major Frere, as I live ! "

" Pierpoint ! " answered the major, equally surprised.

"No less. But where in heaven's name have you dropped from ? Looking out for some employment I suppose. Command of the Bashi-Bazouks ? army service corps ? land transport corps? contractors' robbery corps? Damme, you might have the choice of half a dozen corps. Let's form a corps ourselves. Call it Frere's corps, and I'll join it. I'll come and be your subaltern, as I was in the old days. Good fun, after all, wasn't it, in that old company? I wish I was back in it. I do from the bottom of my heart. How long do you stay? Are you living in town? Come and dine with me some day before you go? When? Name your own day, and we'll dine here at the Rag."

Such a torrent, and it came out so fast, that the major had no chance of putting in a word.

"I've only brought my boy up to town. He's to have a commission in the 145th. Alured," said the major to his son, "let me introduce you to Captain Pierpoint, an old brother officer of mine."

The stranger took off his hat, and made Alured a flourishy sort of bow, which the boy hardly knew how to take—feeling uncertain whether this was the proper thing to do, or whether Captain Pierpoint was only chaffing him.

"Your father's sub. once upon a time,

Mr. Frere; and a very taut hand he was too, I can tell you. Ah, major, I shouldn't mind having it all over again, though."

"What are you doing with yourself now?" asked Frere.

"Nothing. Kicking my heels about, waiting for the off-chance."

"What chance?"

"You know I've been next to old Moynehan's estates and title these years past. I'm heir presumptive still. But the old beggar has married again just to spite me. He hates me like the mischief—always did."

"Whom has he married?"

"Handsome young woman enough, one of the Rivière lot. Not much tin, I believe; but a fine, straight, up-standing young girl. The old ass met Lord Rivière and his daughters down at Baymouth, and no doubt they helped to wheel about his bath-chair, and otherwise kootooed to him. But I call it devilish hard lines on me."

"It serves you right, for looking out for dead men's shoes. But, perhaps, there'll be no children, or only daughters."

"That's like you, Frere. You give me a 'nasty one,' and try to smooth it down in the same breath."

"I wish you luck, Pierpoint."

"I know you do, but I hope it will come soon, for I'm going to the devil—hands down." Then he laughed carelessly, and there was a pause. "Well," at last, "good-day to you, major. Won't you have anything? sherry and bitters, no? Bad example? All right; but he'll learn everything—fast enough. I hope all the same you'll come and feed, and bring the youngun. Engaged every night? Rubbish. I know better. But I do hope we shall meet again before you leave town. Good-bye. My best wishes for the young gentleman."

When they were out of earshot the father remarked—

"How people do change! I remember Pierpoint a smooth-faced lad like yourself, Alured; now he is quite a man about town."

Alured pondered a good deal over his father's speech, wondering what the expression "man about town" might mean exactly.

From the tone in which his father had spoken it was evidently a term of reproach. And yet there was nothing in Pierpoint's appearance to call for adverse criticism. Indeed, as to his outward man he was splendid. His coat—these were the days of "Noah's arks,"—reached to his heels, his hat was of the glossiest, his boots perfection, his gloves new and well-fitting. If such were the adjuncts of a man about town, Alured thought that he too would like to be a man about town. Already he began to be glad that his father had bought him a hat.

"Pierpoint always lived extremely fast," the major continued; "and we never knew where he got his money exactly. Hand to mouth, I suppose. But he seems to be 'keeping it up' still."

The tell-tale wrinkles round about the corners of the eyes and an occasional tremor in the hand spoke volumes to an old campaigner like the major.

After this meeting, father and son proceeded to walk the streets according to the custom of country cousins; flattening their noses against every shop window, as they gazed with admiration upon the display within. In this respect, the major was as young as his son. He had served so much abroad, that London had never lost its glitter in his eyes. He looked upon it as the centre of all that was great and good, and extended his worship even to the shop windows. After all, except to an inveterate *flâneur*, these shops are always charming. There is something new to be seen each day. Picture succeeds picture; photograph, photograph. Attenborough exhibits new vases daily; Fortnum and Mason new sugar-plums. The haberdashers, with an eye for colour, illuminate their plate-glass with a blaze of brightness: to-day blue for the boat-race, to-morrow Denmark red, in honour of a royal wedding. Foreign shops are crowded with gorgeous exotic produce—Algerian jewellery, Chinese jars and Japanese fans, Spanish rugs and Austrian blankets, Danish pottery and brilliant bonnets from our allies across the Channel. What wonder that the simple pair wandered up and down Regent Street and Piccadilly, feasting their eyes on all they saw? Presently the gas flooded every corner with garish light, and the scene grew not unlike the tinsel-beplastered "dazzling halls" of a Christmas extravaganza. But it was now time to dine. So they adjourned to an eating-house in the neighbourhood of their lodgings, where they dined off the joint, with cabinet pudding and Cheddar cheese to follow. After this, to the pit of the Adelphi, where Madame Celeste, as "Janet Pride," appealed in her pathetic foreign English to all that was impressionable in Alured's sensitive young heart. Then when his tears were dry, they went into "Evans's," and eat smoking-hot kidneys, and mammoth potatoes, while Herr von Joel whistled on a stick, or a choir of tuneful boys sang the "Hardy Norseman," or "Au bord de la Duran—cé," or "number one hundred and forty-five in the book."

It had been a glorious day for Alured—full of endless changes and surprising novelties. The lad sat at the foot of his bed, when he got back to Northumberland Street, and revelled in the crowd of new ideas that had been that day presented to him. If this was the beginning, how would it all end? People who were cynical said the world was all hollowness and mockery, all in it vanity and vexation of spirit. "It does not seem so to me," thinks Alured. "It is a beautiful world, and London is its greatest wonder." He sat and dreamed on till his father shouted to him to ask him why he did not put out his light. He roused himself then, and tumbled into bed, nothing loth, to sleep the sleep of innocent sixteen.

But next day, and for several days following, Alured saw little of the pleasures of town. It behoved him to stick close to his books; and by the time he was due at Sandhurst, he had mastered, thanks to judicious cramming, a vast amount of information that was never likely to be of use to him. Strings of dry dates, abstract formulas, and very crude notions on fortification. He was stuffed as full as a force-meat ball.

"Don't touch me, father," he said, laughing, "or I shall go off: I'm loaded to the muzzle."

"I'm sure I hope you've not overdone it," replied his father, rather pathetically. "But do you really think you'll pass?" This was for the fiftieth time of asking.

"I shall, if I don't burst: my head feels very tight."

"You're not going to be ill? Your mother——"

"Not I. But you mustn't talk to me, father. My ideas will get disarranged, or I shall drop some of my facts by mistake."

This was in the train, as they journeyed to the nearest station to Sandhurst. The carriage was full of young men on the same errand as Alured. They were all intent on the coming examination; one was refreshing his memory by reading "Chepmell's History" through; another was complaining bitterly that he knew nothing of logarithms.

"I'll teach you logarithms in half a jiffey," volunteered Alured kindly; "at least, as much as you'll want."

"Will you? You *are* a brick."

The lesson commenced without delay, and was continued in the waiting-room at the College, till Protheroe, the ignoramus, felt strong enough to face the examiners.

"I'm sure you'll pass now," said the major, admiringly, to Alured. The schoolmaster was not abroad in his day, and he had not learnt logarithms himself. The erudition of his son seemed something stupendous. But in truth Alured's success was never in doubt from the first. When his turn came, he followed the orderly down the bare, whitewashed, echoing corridor to the board-room,—a lofty place, lighted from above, and filled with books and talk and people. There was something rather terrible in the ordeal, now the supreme moment had arrived. Alured was strange, too, to the brusqueness of military etiquette, and was taken aback by the gruff greeting of the colonel who superintended operations. But they could not puzzle him. Not even the cross-grained French master, nor yet Doctor Clayton with his cross-questioning in recondite history. It was all plain sailing till he reached one point,—one where he had never dreamt of difficulty.

The surgeon had doubts whether he ought to pass Mr. Frere as fit for service.

"You don't mean that, sir?" said Alured, anxiously.

"I do. It's not that you are unsound."

"Unsound, indeed!"

"Allow me to proceed, young gentleman." The surgeon of the Royal Military College was a dry old stick, who had weathered a dozen epidemics in the West Indies, and laughed at "liver." "It's not that you are unsound. I observe that your respiration is good; your heart regular in its action; you are free from varix, serious rupture, and all internal complaints, and as yet have no decided tendency to phthisis. You are indeed perfectly healthy, Mr. Frere. My only objection is that your constitution is still unformed."

"I am past sixteen."

"You have perhaps read Dr. Parkes on Military Hygiene? or Jackson on the Formation of Armies? or Baron Larrey's reports? No? They are worth studying. You will find that all authorities coincide in one point—in fixing the age at which the recruit is considered fit to undergo the hardships of military service. They agree that the very earliest limit is eighteen."

"But I'm not a recruit,—I'm an officer."

"You'll find yourself in the same box with the recruit, Mr. Frere, out there," said the old doctor, half smiling. Next moment he was gravely smoothing his chin with his hand, then the bald patch on his head, as if hand-rubbing would bring conviction to his doubting brain. "Um—ah—I hardly know what to do. Why can't you wait?"

"All the fun will be over——"

"It's a pity to baulk your ardour—I won't. It will be time enough when you are actually under orders for foreign or active service for the medical officer to interfere."

"You have passed, Mr. Frere," said the colonel at length, holding out his paw to the bright-faced lad, an honour he seldom vouchsafed to candidates for commission. "I congratulate you—you're very young. So much the better,—I was younger when I began."

It was all over, except to communicate the glad news to Major Frere, who, with anxious steps, paced the hall outside the board-room.

"I hope, my boy, you will be as successful through life as in this your first step. Trust in God always. Tell the truth, and behave like a gentleman: you can't go wrong then."

CHAPTER IV.

STARTING.

> "Ther mayst thou see devising of harneis,
> So uncouth and so rich, and wrought so wele,
> Of goldsmithry, of brouding, and of steele;
> The sheldes brighte, testeres, and trappures,
> Gold-hewen helmes, hauberkes, cote armures."
> CHAUCER: *The Knighte's Tale.*

IN those busy times, government offices worked rapidly. Three days later, when the major and Alured were eating their breakfast in Northumberland Street, the *Times* was brought in, containing the previous night's Gazette. In it they read:—

"145th Foot.—Alured Frere, Gent., to be ensign without purchase, vice Robert Frere, killed in action."

"So soon!" cried the major, with a sigh. Gall mingled with his joy, as he saw the names of Robert and Alured side by side. "But I did not expect it for another fortnight at the earliest."

"Let me look at it, father;" and Alured read the words over and over again, till they danced before his eyes.

"I must go and see Hastings about getting you transferred."

"Transferred!"

"Yes, my boy. I promised your mother to get you into a regiment not serving in the Crimea."

"Do you mean that I am not to go to the Crimea?"

"Remember your mother, Alured."

The boy sat silent for a time; then he asked, "Who is Hastings?"

"A friend of mine at the Horse Guards. He has a good deal of interest with Sir Octavius Wilberforce, the Military Secretary, you know."

"Does it depend upon the Military Secretary, father?"

"Yes, of course. But you'll soon learn the routine of these things."

Sooner than his father thought, indeed. Alured now, for the first time, was to show himself a boy of some character and determination. He resolved to make his way in person to Sir Octavius, and to beg that he might not be prevented from going to the war. Naturally he kept his plan secret from his father; but no sooner was the major's back turned than Alured set forth on his momentous errand.

Although a perfect stranger to the streets of London, Alured boldly asked his way to the Horse Guards the moment he left the door of his lodgings; and, as the distance between Northumberland Street and Whitehall is not great, nor the journey intricate, he soon found himself within the hallowed precincts. Passing the mounted sentries, once more he inquired. "The Military Secretary's? Over there, under the arch. The same as the Commander-in-Chief's. Door to the right."

Ringing the ponderous office bell, Alured, with a sinking heart, waited to be admitted. They kept him a long time, so that he had leisure to look about him. The arcade was a thoroughfare constantly crowded with people, who swept by the mammoth lifeguardsman keeping watch and ward, as if they were ocean waves and he a fossil of the past. But he was a living soldier, of real flesh and blood. His limbs were not always stony and rigid. Occasionally he performed to a select audience of brats and a bewitched nursemaid, who looked up to him as a colossal monolith of the King of England, the varied programme of a dismounted dragoon on sentry. Now changing, flamingo-like, from one leg to the other; now extending one by one the fingers of his gloved left hand; now varying the position of his carbine, which he lightly carried as if in his sight it were a toy, or he took a short turn, a yard or two at the most, merely to give him an opportunity of throwing back his shoulders or making his spurs jingle. A very stalwart and imposing warrior, who so absorbed Alured's attention that the door was open long before hs was aware of it.

"Is Sir Octavius Wilberforce at home?"

"This his not 'is private residence. It's 'is horfice."

"Is he here? Can I see him?"

"Is your name down?"

"Ought it to have been put down first? I'm sorry, but it's an urgent case."

"Hair you a horficer?"

"Yes," answered Alured, proudly.

The ink was hardly dry yet on his commission.

The porter's manner underwent a change.

"You'd better see Mr. Snell, sir; top story; left 'and side; second door. Confidential clerk arranges all the interviews."

Alured passed through the portals. How many others, great men and small, had trodden those steps, and he came there to take his chance of the future like the rest! A crabbed old messenger met him on the top of the stairs, and scanned him doubtingly from head to foot.

"Now *is* your name on the list? No? Then you *can't* see Sir Octavius."

He got quite querulous and angry on the spot. Not a little of the insolence of office had crystallized around this feeble old creature, during the many years he had acted as buffer to save the great man his master from importunity.

"I shall go and see Mr. Snell," said Alured, bursting into a laugh, as he bounded up the staircase. When he returned, his petition granted, he found the messenger still standing spell-bound where he had left him.

"Go in and take a chair," stammered out the old fellow feebly, as he showed the way to the waiting-room. There was no chair vacant, for the boy found himself among a crowd of suppliants. The Military Secretary, great dispenser of patronage and promotion, has always a large *clientèle.* That widow, in deepest black, has come to beg a commission for her fatherless boy. Next her is Sir Hector Mainwearing, leaning on his crutch, and glaring ferociously at every new comer. He is old enough almost to remember Marlborough, or Julius Cæsar, yet he wants a billet. "Employment, sir; active employment! What do they mean by putting me on the shelf? I'm as fit as a fiddle." But several of the strings are cracked. One of the gallant old fellow's legs is somewhere in Belgium, and the other is swathed hebdomadally in flannel. Within a week or two you will hear that he has been found dead in a chair at his club. Most of the others are grey-haired captains or lieutenants, come to beg promotions. One or two are skulkers, like Delafield, who saw two days of it "at the front," and won't go back. He is the biggest fire-eater in the room, but he is seeking all the same to stay at home and keep his skin whole. Alured shrank before all these strange faces, and blushed as he tried to hide in one corner of the room, behind the great press, full of obsolete correspondence, which was its only ornament. But Sir Hector's fierce though watery eye was upon him, dragging him out of his obscurity, as a pin does a periwinkle from its shell. That angry eye seemed reproaching the lad for being so young. There was just a tinge of comfort in the widow's compassionate glance, who more than once looked Alured's way. She was thinking perhaps of her own son, and wondered whether they were not a little alike in age and feature. The others sat whispering together in groups of two or three, but Alured felt convinced they were talking of him. Every moment he seemed to grow more shy and uncomfortable. Then by degrees the room thinned, applicant after applicant had audience, and at last it came to Alured's turn.

"Mr. Frere—Sir Octavius!" cried the messenger, introducing him, and throwing the door wide open.

Next minute our hero was alone with the great man.

"Well, boy."

The general spoke roughly, but not unkindly.

"What can I do for you? Want a commission? Who are you? Where do you belong? Left school yet—hey what! what! what?" His voice was so cheery and kind that Alured found courage to look up. He saw a red-faced, rather portly gentleman, with very white whiskers, standing with his legs wide apart before the fire.

"If you please, sir, I'm—I'm Mr.—, I mean Ensign Frere, of the 145th."

"Frere!—Frere!—Frere!—ah, I remember. Well?"

"I've been gazetted to the 145th, and my mother does not wish me to go to the war, and I do. Oh, please, sir, do let me go."

"Why the 145th is at the war," said Sir Octavius, good-naturedly. "You'll have to go fast enough. Don't be afraid. Hey, what, what, what?"

"It's not that. My father is trying to get me

transferred, and I don't want to be transferred—I want to go to the war."

"Quite right too. So you shall! so you shall! so you shall! Gad, I like your spirit. Who's your father?"

"Major Frere."

"Of the —th once. Good officer. I knew him. Hope you'll be like him. You needn't be alarmed, Mr. Frere. There are no vacancies in any regiments except those at the Crimea. When your father asks he is sure to be refused."

"Thank you, sir. I——."

"Anything else I can do for you?"

"No."

"Good-bye then. Hope you'll live to succeed me here some day. I wish you luck, my boy," said the general, extending one hand cordially from beneath his coat tail to be shaken, and Alured left the Horse Guards in great glee.

Should he tell his father at once where he had been? There was no deceitfulness about the lad, and it pained him rather when he thought that he had been acting an underhand part. He could not bear to keep his secret to himself. His father had a right to know what had happened. So directly Alured got back to Northumberland Street he made a clean breast of it.

"If you please, father, I have been—I have been—to the Horse Guards."

"To the Horse Guards?" replied the major, much surprised.

"I have seen and spoken to Sir Octavius."

Major Frere's eyes opened wider and wider at each announcement.

"He says it will be no use to ask for me to be transferred. That there are no vacancies except in the Crimean regiments."

"Did you think of your mother, Alured?"

"I know it was wrong of me, father; but I want to go so much!"

I do not think Major Frere was displeased at this exhibition of independent spirit on the part of his son. It consoled him somewhat for the uncertain future, to find the lad already plucky and self-reliant.

"But I must try what I can do, Alured. I promised your mother."

He tried; but to no purpose. And it became necessary to make preparations for launching this young craft, "Alured Frere, Self, master," into the billows of the world.

Messrs. Jobson & Co., that old established firm of Bond Street, were commissioned to provide the young man's outfit. These world-renowned tailors had made uniforms for the Freres for generations. The Freres, for ages back, father and son, had been soldiers. It would have been better, perhaps, for the prosperity of the family, if here and there some energetic cadet, had taken to another line. One or two successful soap or sugar boilers, a retail tobacconist, or an occasional grocer, might have done something to swell the revenues of the house of Frere. As it was, there was often a scarcity of money in the clan; for the military profession, if honourable, is certainly not lucrative. After some years' existence on the salary of a railway guard or an irresponsible clerk, weighted with large disbursements from his private fortune to purchase himself promotion, a general or a colonel who has grown grey in the service, finds the provision made by a grateful country so limited, that the business of a decent crossing-sweeper would be a valuable addition to his income. Major Frere often said that he wished his father had apprenticed him to a respectable tailor like Jobson.

Messrs. Jobson & Co. had measured Robert Frere, senior, and Robert Frere, junior, for their regimentals; and now little Mr. Hands, the managing-partner of the firm, began to dance round Alured with a tape, taking the lad's proportions for one of these new-fangled "toonics," which both he and the major condemned.

"Don't like the change, major, sir, eh?" asked the little man.

"Not I. I'm a conservative. The coatee was good enough to my mind; and they'll never invent anything half so handsome as the epaulet. This tunic—it looks like a short night-gown."

"You're quite right, major. There was a customer of ours 'ere this morning, major, sir —14, 42;—a customer, Colonel Angersteen —27, 11 *and* a half. He's been appointed queen's eddycong, and he came to be measured

STARTING.

for one of these noo toonics — 9, 13, 22 — to go to court in, and he said positively, positively, he said he couldn't appear in it. You see, major, as you will remember, the old dress was very 'ansum, and now there's nothing but the agalett, and the coat is long, like a huntsman's coat, and full in the skirt, and no other ornament whatsoever."

"Too loose?" This was to Alured. "Oh, it don't do to be skimpy. And you'll fill it out, sir. You'll be like your father one of these days—broad; must give him room, eh, major? Room to grow, Mr. Frere," patronisingly. "You'll be wider in the chest, I'll be bound, when you come to be measured for your queen's eddycong's coat. The same regiment, major, as," went on the garrulous little man, shaking his head mournfully. "Ah, yes, *of* course. We saw it in the *Gazette*. It was very sad, major, very sad." He was referring now to Robert Frere's death. "What a terrible action that was! I assure you, sir, we felt it severely."

General actions operate with wonderful effect in simplifying a London tailor's ledger.

There was no end to the flow of Mr. Hands' loquacity. At one moment, he was lachrymose, the next full of his small jokes. How well did Alured remember in after-life, the little man and the little room off the shop, where he had swelled out his chest and tried to look so big the day he was measured for his first red coat. There was no end of mirrors, tall cheval glasses, and others, fastened into the wall, so as to give every conceivable view of the figure. Here he saw face, and back beyond, at the same time. Here a perfect regiment of legs twinkled away one beyond the other into space. All about were strewn the materials of military greatness, the pomp and circumstance that gild the pill. Heaps of garments ready to be tried on, encumbered all the chairs; a brilliant patchwork, with gold lace and sparkling buttons, ready to be sewn in. On the mantelpiece were ranged half-a-dozen "forage" caps, of different patterns; staff, diceboard, and peakless cavalry caps. An old wardrobe in one corner, was crammed full of the finery of a by-gone age. Hideous helmets, over which curled a long furry feather, as thick and bushy as a Newfoundland's tail; a militia shako, five times wider at the top than at the bottom, and festooned with a chain cable of tarnished silver; the dolman of a hussar, a horse-artilleryman's jacket, from which the blaze of gold had burnt out in the lapse of years; crimson and purple shabraques, swords, scabbards, sabretaches, shoe-brushes. In the centre of the shrine stood little Mr. Hands. Major Frere on the hearthrug, smiling approval. Through the window, high up in the wall, came as much of the scant yellow London light as could be spared from between the dark dingy chimney-tops and blackened gable ends of the houses that hemmed in the shop behind; and in this dusky twilight, the lad stood, trying to appear calm and collected as each new proof of his importance was thrust upon him.

By-and-by, the measuring over, they proceeded through the work-rooms to some underground stores, where there was endless choice, among portmanteaus, valises, camp-beds, and barrack furniture. For everything was to be provided by Messrs. Jobson & Co., except the lad's sword, which was presented to him by Sir Malcolm Macgregor, one of his father's oldest friends, and Alured's portrait, which no tailor could have painted. This last was a masterpiece of M. Bergmann, a celebrated artist in chalks; for an oil painting was thought too expensive, and photography was still in its infancy. At Monsieur Bergman's, in Portland Street, a boy from Messrs. Jobson's met them with a black bag from which the new uniform coat was produced for the sitting. This work of art was pronounced by all judges to be a most faithful likeness; and it is still preserved among the family portraits of the Freres. A sketchy drawing, but bold in its outlines, and much intelligence has been imparted to the bright young face as it smiles upon you from the grey paper.

Thus employed, the days slipped quickly by. These preparations kept Alured in a whirl of excitement, and there were other calls upon the lad's time. He had to be taken round and exhibited to his relatives; for he was the hope of the family now. So he ran down to Clapham to be made much of by his mother's uncle, and to Hastings where aunts and cousins nearly tore the handsome lad in pieces. He was introduced to all his father's soldier friends. To-night he dined with General This at his club, the next with Colonel That in the Albany, or he went with his father to a fortress town not far from London, where the commandant fêted him, and he heard drums and bugles play for the first time in his life. It was all supreme enjoyment to Alured. His letters home, chiefly to Lilian, his special favourite, were filled with all he saw and did, and the little bedroom in Northumberland Street was becoming crammed with the presents he had collected for his father to take back to the dear ones at Scaggleton.

But the time approached when Alured's leave expired. It was necessary to prepare for the real start. Major Frere knew well how important it was that his son's debut should be good in his new profession. It would not have raised Alured's character among his new comrades if he had been taken to join "under escort." So it was arranged that the major was to accompany him to Euston Square, and no farther. When the luggage had been labelled, the through-ticket obtained, and the lad fairly bestowed in a first-class carriage, the father meant to cut the leading strings, and set his son adrift to shift for himself.

Two days in advance of the time when he was due at Ballybanagher, where the depot of his regiment then lay, Alured drove with his father to the station. They were in plenty of time for the Irish night-mail. It was the major's custom to be always much too soon for anything he had to do. Now, having some forty minutes to spare, they paced together the grand but cheerless hall at Euston Square, and circled round and round the young man's baggage which his father would not allow out of his sight. It was here, as he gazed upon the trucks loaded with his belongings, that Alured began to realize his new position. The bullock-trunks, brand-new and shining, bore on their varnished backs his name and titles in full,—large white letters on a black ground,—proclaiming to all the world that this was "Alured Frere, Esq., of the 145th Regiment," bound to Ballybanagher. This noble superscription almost took away his breath as he read it. He wondered whether the bystanders were aware that it was *he* who was an officer in the army, Alured Frere by name; and in his doubts he seized his sword-case, and hugged it under his arm, as if to *afficher* himself to all the world. But the pride ebbed away out of him pretty fast when all these fine things had been put away in the van, and he found himself ensconced in the corner of the carriage bidding adieu to his father. He clung rather nervously to the kind hand that seemed, nevertheless, to be thrusting him away. Major Frere was outwardly composed. He was fearful lest by an anxious look or clouded brow he might damp his boy's fresh spirit and eager ardour; but inwardly his heart smote him not a little. How young and childish Alured looked! with such a smooth boyish face, such honest, innocent eyes, a figure so slight and unformed! Was this stripling fit to start upon his own bottom, to face the world, and if needs be fight it? To be exposed to hardships, wounds, temptations, trials? Surely the father's heart was sore. At that moment his first-born's fate rose freshly to his mind, and in his ears was ringing his wife's pleading voice, begging so piteously that her second son might be spared.

But it was too late now to withdraw. Besides, had not he himself gone forth from the nest at the same tender age to try the strength of his wings? Why anticipate evil? The major hoped for the best, and by way of farewell, spoke a short sharp common-place word.

"Good-bye, now, my dear boy. Be sure you ask for hot water things if you feel the cold; and you'll write, won't you, from Dublin, or wherever you can first? Now—" and there was a short pause, during which each looked in the other's eyes, a long unflinching gaze—"Alured; good-bye, God bless you. I know you will do well." A warm pressure of the hand was all Alured's reply; for there was a great lump in his throat, which, with all his bravery, he could not gulp down. No more was said. The bell was ringing, there was a banging of doors, the guard's whistle was blown shrilly above the din, and the train began to move slowly off leaving Major Frere, to Alured's eyes, a dim figure on the platform, scarce recognisable for the mist that obscured—well, let us say the carriage window.

Then the engine gave a fierce snort, and taking the bit between its teeth, rattled off at lightning speed, forth from the gas-lit station out into the dark cheerless night.

CHAPTER V.

FAIRLY OFF.

Enter Pistol.
Pistol. Qui va là.
K. Henry. A friend.
Pistol. Discuss unto me—Art thou an officer, or art thou base, common, and popular?
K. Henry. I am a gentleman of a company.
Henry V.

"LIKE a young bear, eh?" said a voice by-and-by at Alured's elbow. But the remark had to be repeated before it roused the lad from his thoughts.

"Like a young bear, eh? wid all your troubles beforr you."

"I beg your pardon," said Alured abstractedly. "Did you speak to me?"

"I did that, me bhoy. And whhere might you be bound forr?"

Alured did not like this cross-examination. He had been particularly cautioned against making friends with strangers. Stories of card-sharpers and decoys crossed his mind at once, so he answered as he thought stiffly and with dignity.

"I am going to join my regiment."

"Och murther! and would they be sending a wee slip of a chap like you to the bloody wars? What a cruel shame."

A hot flush passed over the lad's face as he replied, indignantly,—

"That's my business. Besides, my father was younger by two years than I am when he entered the service."

"Mighty useful you'll be out yonder. For you'll be going to the Crimay, of coorse?"

"Yes; my regiment is there. I hope to get out before the war is over."

His interlocutor burst into a loud laugh, which made Alured angrier than ever. But the first speaker was immediately checked by another passenger, evidently his companion— there were only the three people in the carriage.

"Leave the young gentleman alone, Shamus. Where the divil are yer manners. I hope, sir," went on the new voice to Alured, "you won't mind him. He was brought up in a hedge school, and his father wouldn't pay the extra sod of turf for good breeding. He's always full of his jokes, though they're bad at the best. Might I ask whether yer going over to ould Ireland? ye are?"

"Yes; to Ballybanagher."

"I dare say yer strange to this line. I shall be very glad to be of any use with your baggage and all that."

Alured hugged his ticket close, and looked anxiously up to the rack to see if his hat-box and sword-case were safe. This was another and a more insidious attack he thought upon himself and his belongings.

"We're going as far as Westland Row—Dublin I mean—and we'll be proud to do the honours for you to the ould country."

"Thank you very much," replied Alured coldly—after which there was a pause in the conversation. Presently the others began to talk about butter, bacon, and pigs, thereby revealing themselves and their calling. From this they diverged to a discussion about accents and brogues. The last of which Alured remembered was a remark from Shamus, a

Kerry man, that the "Cārk brōg was a vurry bād brōg." But not even these interesting topics, added to the jarring motion of the carriage, could overcome his drowsiness. He nodded off; first in fitful dozes, then into a long deep slumber, from which he was awakened by his fellow-travellers, who were covering him up with wrappers, and endeavouring, kind souls, to make him warm and comfortable.

"You'll be as snug as a bug in a rug," said Shamus. "Now take a drap of the craytur—"

But Alured declined the profferred flask of whisky, and within a minute was again sound asleep.

The passage across from Holyhead to Kingstown was a newer and sadder experience to the young soldier. Here his fellow-travellers again stood his friend; and when he bade them farewell at Westland Row, his conscience smote him for thinking evil of their good intentions. Once more alone, he traversed "Dublin city," and took train again for Ballybanagher. The manners and customs of the Irish struck him as peculiar, but his mind was too full just then to allow of his taking exact notes of all that passed about him. One incident, however, made some impression, and that was the conduct of a gentleman who occupied the same compartment. Once when the train came to a stoppage, this person threw down the window with a bang, and thrusting out his head cried,—

" Hwhats that ?"

" Kee-lucan," replied a porter, promptly.

" I whill NOT," answered the passenger, shutting up the window as he had opened it; and Alured never was able to guess the nature of their colloquy.

Three hours' journey brought them to Ballaborris, the station advertised for Ballybanagher. As he got out on the platform by himself, Alured began to feel very friendless and sick at heart. An Irish wayside station by the light of a grey wintry day is by no means a scene to exhilarate and cheer the spirit. A sensation of utter loneliness settled down on his heart as he looked around at the dull landscape: dreary bogs stretching to meet at the horizon a leaden sky barred with lines of blurred and ragged clouds. He thought himself the last living thing in the world. The train had rattled away and left him, alone, deserted, as if it had been been a shipful of mutineers and he their skipper, whom they had abandoned on an uninhabited island. Almost involuntarily a half-stifled shout escaped from him, as a sleeper weighted by some choking incubus finds relief in an indistinct cry.

"Hi! here! hillo!"

His voice gave him courage, and now for the first time he became aware that there was a house near at hand. It was the station, and in the waning light he made out one single figure moving amidst a heap of black bales.

It was the porter busy with Alured's baggage, who having heard the other's voice came up to speak.

"Is it far you're going, captain."

In Ireland every officer is a captain, just as every body of troops, from a brigade to a corporal's guard, is an army.

"To Ballybanagher," replied young Frere.

"Faix, yer honour won't get to Ballybanagher this night."

"Can't I get a conveyance of some kind?"

"Sorra a convaniency. Pat Morrisy's cart is the only thing on wheels these ten miles, and that's away in the bog wid the peat."

"Is there nowhere I can put up? No village? No inn?"

"Sorra a put up. Lasteways there's the widow Clusky's shebeen house; but she'd be hard put to to make out a bed for you."

"Then what am I to do? Say something—suggest something, man!" cried Alured, seizing him rather roughly by the arm.

"Aisy, captain, aisy."

"Does no one ever come to this God-forsaken place? What's the good of a station? How does anybody ever get anywhere? How do they get to Ballybanagher?"

"They never get this way, at all, captain; sorra a haporth of them. They go by Athenmore, and cross by coach eight miles."

"What am I to do then? Walk?"

"Is it walk? and the country as wild as—Holy Vargin!"

Alured sat down again, on his boxes, in despair.

"I must be at Ballybanagher before the morning."

"Go round by Athenmore then, captain. Try the short cut."

"Is there a short cut?"

"Yes, shure. Through Doblin. There's a train up in a minute," and the porter laughed at his own ingenuity. "The longest way round's the shortest way there, and I've found it often enough—when I try the road home across the bog with my skin full of whisky."

Alured was half disposed to follow this advice, but he could not part with his baggage, and the porter said it was too heavy to go by express. Just then the train arrived.

Strange to say, there proved to be several passengers for Ballybanagher station, notwithstanding its deserted appearance. An oldish man, small, rather wizened, wrapped up in furs, got out of a first class carriage, followed by a lady of tall and commanding figure. Presently a servant in livery came from the back part of the train, and a lady's-maid, laden with cloaks, and carrying a large dressing-bag. The party quite took possession of the station.

Even the stolid porter grew abjectly obsequious, and tried to extemporize something of a reception,—would his lordship do this, or that, and would his lordship's own man give his orders about the baggage.

"Hasn't the carriage come?" asked the lady rather shortly.

"Troth, I never seed it my lady, ma'am," replied the porter.

"My dear," she went on to her husband, "that coachman is not to be depended upon in the least. You really must see about a change."

"If this sort of thing is to happen often, I quite agree with you."

"Barkins recommended the man for punctuality too. I hope you do not find it very cold," she said, her tone changing quickly from annoyance to one of great solicitude.

"Av ye plaze to come in beyant," suggested the porter, "I'll heighten up the fire wid a sod or two."

"Thank you, my good man," said his lordship. "Go in, my lady. I'd rather take a brisk turn; that carriage has quite numbed my feet."

Presently he came to where her ladyship sat before the fire.

"My dear, we have company in our misfortunes."

"Indeed. Who is it?"

"A young gentleman who is going to join at Ballybanagher. I've been talking to him. You never saw such a shrimp of a fellow."

"And how does he propose to get to Ballybanagher?" asked her ladyship, cosily shrugging her shoulders, and cuddling up her hands in her great muff.

"He asked me whether I thought it was too far to walk; the porter here has been humbugging him about the insecurity of the road. Shall we give him a seat in the carriage?"

"As you please, my dear."

"You don't object?"

"I? Why should I? The carriage is big enough; and if it wasn't, he could sit in the rumble with Hedger."

"You wouldn't object if you were to see him. It's worth your while—it is really—to come out and have a look at this great warrior."

"I'm much too comfortable here to move away on any voyage of discovery."

"Then I'll bring him in to you."

"Oh, no; don't do that; I'll come."

It was enough to smite the strongest heart with pity to see the poor little chap sitting perturbed and disconsolate upon top of his baggage. He was tired of walking up and down, and had retreated to hide among his boxes when the strangers invaded the station. He was now debating in his own mind whether he could not bivouac then and there, where he was. It was some time before he became aware of the spectators that were gazing, seemingly amused, upon his troubled face and dejected air. When he did look up, it was the lady who caught his attention, as she leant upon her husband's arm, with her hands clasped in her muff, outside of which was visible, just a rim of white wrist encircled by a ponderous bracelet. It was a handsome countenance, with proudly curving features and well-cut aristocratic lips. Alured looked up into her face, and then sunk his eyes, full of dancing motes, dazzled, as if he had been staring at the sun.

She spoke first.

"May we offer you a seat in our carriage, Mr. Frere?"

Alured jumped as she mentioned his name. They knew him, then? Poor little fool! Was he not sitting amidst his baggage? Surrounded by those same tell-tale boxes that had flattered his pride at Euston Square with their staring manifesto of his name and calling?

"We are passing by Ballybanagher, and can drop you at the barracks," she continued.

"Oh, thank you so much!" The boy's cheeks flushed scarlet, partly with shyness, partly with joy at the prospect of deliverance. "But—but—I'm afraid—I shall crowd you."

Poor Alured; he had been ransacking his brain for something fine, but the proper words would not come.

"Not in the least," said his lordship, courteously; "the carriage is a large one, and we shall be delighted if you will come with us,—that is if the carriage turns up. But at present we are in the same predicament as yourself."

"There are the wheels, now, I think," cried my lady. "Where is Hedger? Pick out the boxes I require, Hedger; and we can take a portmanteau for you, too, Mr. Frere. Not more I'm afraid. The rest of your things can come on by the cart to-morrow."

Within a few minutes, Alured found the scene pleasantly changed. Instead of the dreary station, a warm, soft-cushioned, roomy carriage; instead of solitude, friends, or at least kind strangers, as companions, and one of them a charming woman.

He had taken his seat before the owner of the carriage, because his lordship insisted on it, but Alured had manners enough to place himself with his back to the horses. He was then offered, courteously, the seat next my lady, but this he would by no means accept. Very soon his lordship fell asleep in his corner, and left his wife to converse undisturbed with Alured Frere.

All the conversation did not amount to much. Alured was perfectly tongue-tied. He had not the faintest idea what to talk about; no notion what subjects would please her. Quite unversed in the ways of the great world, and unacquainted with the distinctions of rank, he was awestruck before this great lady, who, for all he knew, might be a duchess. Shyness is the resultant of intense self-consciousness and ignorance. Alured felt himself driven by these two forces into a very abyss of *mauvaise honte*. He began to be tormented with the thought that she must despise him as a silly little fool. His terror and his discomfort increased each instant that the silence continued. Presently, to his inflamed imagination, the corner of the carriage became filled with an awful but beautiful presence—of some goddess enshrined in a cloud of sweet-smelling incense, clothed in splendid robes. He gazed upon the dark depths before him, expecting each instant that a sun of dazzling light would burst forth, and he woke, suddenly, from his trance; roused— by a touch, by a portion of her drapery, light and feathery, brushing past him. Although young and a boy, he was human. There was something in the contact of the smooth, slippery silk that sent a thrill through him; a shiver of pleasure that mingled not unpleasantly with the fears that still oppressed him. A mysterious sympathy was communicated by this *frôlement* of her dress. Almost instinctively he grew more at ease. Just then, too, her voice, soft and caressing in its tones, though perhaps she spoke languidly and without apparent interest, broke the silence and the spell under which he had lain.

" Is my dress much in your way? I fear I am quite smothering you."

" No."

There was another pause, during which she bestowed her folds more to her liking, and drew the wraps closer about her.

" Have you travelled far to-day?"

No doubt she meant to be kind, but her questions were put in a listless, insouciant tone, which quite crushed all Alured's nascent courage.

He replied falteringly—

" I came from London last night."

" And you are going to join all by yourself?"

" Yes."

" At your age?"

"I'm not so very young," Alured said, waxing stout and independent.

"Indeed!" Possibly she anticipated that she was going to be bored with details, for the query was more cold and indifferent than anything she had previously said.

"No; I am past sixteen."

"A very tremendous age, no doubt, Mr. Frere. But most other boys are still at sch—well, Eton at—your age."

"My father began earlier."

"He was a soldier? Pardon my saying it—I thought so. No one but an old soldier would have started you like this, to begin the world all by yourself."

"And my brother was very little older either," said Alured, harping on the same string.

"Is your brother at Ballybanagher to meet you?"

"He is dead. He was killed at Inkerman."

"And now you are going too? I wonder,"—all that was womanly in her woke up to pity at once,—"I wonder how your mother could let you go!"

After this the ice was broken, and she began to question him about his family,—his sisters and his mother especially.

"And what part of the world do you come from, Mr. Frere?"

"From along the east coast. We live at a very out-of-the-way place, of which I dare say you have never heard,—Scaggleton."

"Scaggleton!" she said sharply, starting a little.

"You have never been there surely?"

"Oh yes, I have. Years and years ago. There is an old house under the crags—the Castle I think it is called, or Scaggleton Castle, or some such name; do you know it?"

"Why, that is where we live."

"How odd! Some dear friends of mine lived there, too, once; and I seem to know the place by heart."

"It is such a jolly old house! not really old, you know. It's only a cockney castle, but the turrets and the fortifications make it seem quite real, and the rocks, and Haddock Hole, and that big reef which goes out ever so far when the tide is low?"

He waited for an answer, but none came. What was she thinking about? or was it that she had not heard him? He repeated his question; still no reply. Then he thought he had been talking too much, and lapsed into silence, which lasted some time.

At length she spoke:—

"I beg your pardon, I'm sure, Mr. Frere. It was very rude of me, but I was deep in old times. The memory of Scaggleton is very dear to me," she added, with a sigh. Then with an effort, she roused herself to speak of other things.

"Don't you think you had better come on with us to Moynehan, Mr. Frere—I mean to our house? We will send you back to barracks, if you like, first thing to-morrow."

"I should be very glad, but—but—my father said I was to go straight to barracks, and report myself directly I arrived, and I think I ought to."

The lad was wavering between his duty thus clearly defined by the major, and the fear of seeming ungracious by rejecting the proffered kindness.

"Do you know any one there?"

"Not a soul."

"How are you to manage? You have left all your things at Ballaborris too. You had better come with us."

"Thank you, so much. But if you please, I think—if you will excuse me—I think I will go to the barracks to-night."

"So you shall, Mr. Frere," cried Lady Moynehan, laughing. "It would be a pity to baulk so eager and conscientious a soldier at the very beginning."

There was something so innocent, yet so independent and straightforward about the lad, he was so young, and yet so anxious to do what was right, that he quite won Lady Moynehan's heart.

At the barrack gate the carriage stopped. Lord Moynehan woke up, and bade Mr. Frere good-night. Her ladyship shook hands with him very warmly and kindly, the steps were put up, and the carriage door shut, and he was left alone once more.

Most Irish barracks are built upon the same plan. Built to resist a *coup de main*, they are surrounded by a high, loop-holed wall, flanked by bastions at the angles, and the only ingress is through a tall, substantial gate-way, which is barred and locked at sun-down. Upon this big gate, Alured began, after some hesitation, to hammer with his umbrella.

At the first blow, a stentorian voice within, sang out in a *crescendo* note, "Who *goes* THERE?"

Alured was not aware that he was going anywhere, nor did he quite know what to answer. But continued to knock.

"Who goes there?" was repeated; if anything, in a louder key.

"Frere!" replied Alured, rather timidly. He thought every one would know that he was coming to join; but he was not quite certain whether he ought to have answered, "Frere," or "Alured Frere," or "Mr. Frere," or "Ensign Frere."

"Frere!" replied the voice. "What Frere?"

"Frere, the officer," shouted Alured, goaded to despair.

Then there was a shout of "Gate!" within, and in another minute the light of a bull's-eye was flashed on him through a small window in the wicket.

"Beg your pardon, sir—?" said the sergeant, seeing the slight young figure standing by a portmanteau.

"I have come to join."

"Shall I open the big gate, sir? Have you a car, sir? No?" Mr. Frere was admitted with his portmanteau through the wicket. "I'll send one of the men of the guard with you to the mess, sir," said the sergeant. And at last it seemed as if Alured was at his journey's end, his troubles over, the goal reached.

Yet when the soldier who had accompanied him from the gate, had deposited the trunk upon the ground and disappeared, Alured felt as far from his destination as if he was still at Euston Square. The rooms of the mess-house were all on the ground floor, *en suite*, forming an imposing block. Half a dozen handsome stone steps led to a wide verandah, from which opened doors and windows of the ante-room, the mess-room and billiard-room being at right angles to this external staircase. All the windows were draped with heavy crimson curtains, but a chink here and there betrayed the lights that blazed within. It was past nine o'clock. Dinner must have been long over, but there was a loud hum of voices inside, and occasionally a burst of merriment, laughter, and now and then a shout. Alured sat down on his portmanteau, at the foot of the stone steps, and upbraided himself for so foolishly refusing Lady Moynehan's invitation. For what was he to do now he was actually inside the barracks? He could not remain all night upon those stone steps. Some one would be coming out directly, and would find him there. There was no bell, no knocker. Should he walk in, card in hand, and announce himself? He began to feel it very cold, and the rain was falling heavily. This was the worst phase of all his adventures. But for his own stupidity, he might still be in that comfortable carriage with——

"Who the mischief are *you*, and what are you doing there?"

It was like the explosion of a shell, this voice—a short, sharp report, that sent Alured's heart into his mouth.

"I'm very sorry—I beg pardon. I was waiting—I mean—my name is Frere—I have come to join."

"Come to join! at this time of night! My conscience, you're a rum customer. Golly, what a lark. Hold on a minute—and,—stay, what's your regiment?"

"The 145th," Frere answered, and again was left alone. For the other speaker who had been at the top of the steps, returned to the ante-room.

In a few minutes, another person came out, and descended the steps with outstretched hands.

"Mr. Frere? My name is Davidson,—Captain Davidson of the 145th. Will you come to my quarters? You would like something to eat, perhaps? We'll order it to be sent over by the time you have washed your hands. Is that your box? One of the mess servants will take it over. Come along."

"What kind people there are in the world," thought Alured. In a few minutes more, the forlorn boy was thawing and growing loquacious before Davidson's fire.

CHAPTER VI.

"*THE CUSTOM OF WAR IN LIKE CASES.*"

Re-enter Soldiers with Parolles.
2nd Lord. Hoodman comes ! *Porto tartarossa.*
1st Soldier. He calls for the tortures.
All's Well that Ends Well.

"I'M afraid," said Davidson, "you must have been kept a long time out in the cold. Why did you not come straight in?"

"I did not like to, sir."

"The fact is, you have arrived at a very important moment, that is why you were not noticed sooner. The,"—here he lowered his voice and spoke in a whisper,—"the *general* is here. The country is very unsettled, and he is obliged to travel by night, so that no one may be quite certain ever where he exactly is."

"Indeed, sir." Alured persisted in calling his new friend "sir," without observing the smile that the title, each time, elicited.

"Yes; and he has come for a very sad

reason. Poor Cuthbert,—you know Cuthbert, of the Fusiliers?"

"No."

"Well, he is not a bad chap, but he is to be tried to-night by court-martial. Perhaps you might like to be present?"

Frere said he should like it of all things. His father wished him to lose no opportunity of improving himself in military law and the practice of courts-martial.

"Ah, very proper," remarked Davidson, gravely. "This will be the very thing for you—a capital beginning."

As soon as Alured was ready, and had eaten the food brought over from the mess, they started for the court-house.

The scene about to be described had of course been improvised for Alured's especial benefit; but it was not the first mock trial that Ballybanagher barracks had seen. To while the long winter evenings, the wags of the depot were in the habit of sitting in judgment on their weaker brethren. The offences over which they assumed jurisdiction were rather varied. One young fellow was tried for being

"THE CUSTOM OF WAR IN LIKE CASES." 95

"greedy at dinner," and was sentenced to have no apple tart for three consecutive nights. Another was arraigned for spelling his name with two small ffs at the beginning; a third for absenting himself without leave from the society of his brother officers, and preferring gin and pipes in his own room. As a general rule the culprits fell in with the humour of the thing, and sought by long and specious arguments to prove their innocence. Occasionally one, more than usually cross-grained, "cut up rusty"; but it did not help him much. He was handed over forthwith to the tormentors, who played "sacks at the mill" with him, or "made hay" in his room, or packed up his kit while he was on guard, and directed the boxes to his home, as a gentle hint that he might retire as soon as he thought fit.

Davidson told Alured that as the trial was conducted by special commission, the general himself in the chair, the court sat with closed doors. Permission, however, had been obtained for him to be present, but he must be first sworn to secrecy, and blindfolded before he was admitted. So they covered up his eyes, and led him a dance round the mess-premises; now and then chains were rattled close to his ears, or the dish-covers were dropped, and one ensign with a weak painful voice was told off to groan at stated intervals during Alured's progress. At length he was ushered into the chamber of justice, after much parleying at the outer door, and when the bandage was removed from his eyes he found himself in a lofty room filled with smoke, and not entirely free from an aroma of spirituous drinks. At one end sat an imposing personage, tall, with a great hooked nose and high cheek-bones, the length and solemnity of his face being heightened by the drooping moustaches and sharp pointed imperial. He was on a species of raised dais (a few boards laid on chairs), and was clothed in wide flowing robes,—suspiciously like window curtains. To his right and left sat two others similarly arrayed. In front of them, at a long interval, stood a man in his shirt-sleeves with arms tied behind his back with a rope; and near him, at a small table, was an old gentleman in a wig and long black gown. These five were the prominent figures in the room; but dispersed in

"THE CUSTOM OF WAR IN LIKE CASES." 97

groups around, a number of young men in red jackets lounged and laughed, and from them came the smoke and odour of drink. There was no attempt at decorum among them. When Alured entered they were talking and laughing uproariously. But presently the chief man in the window-curtain spoke, and respectful silence followed.

"Who is this?" asked the general, in a deep and sonorous voice of Davidson, Alured's conductor.

"A newly joined officer, your excellency, who has obtained your permission to witness the proceedings."

"I am aware of it. I would speak with the young man. Let him approach."

Alured was marched to the foot of the dais.

"Your name, young man?"

"Alured Frere."

"The date of your vaccination, a detailed account of your christening, with the godfathers and godmothers who stood, their names and calling, distinctive marks if any, approximate calculation of the united ages of your father, mother, aunts, grand-uncles, cousins german (if any), and a short *résumé* of your own life from the earliest period. Are you prepared with the necessary replies on these questions?"

This was a terrible ordeal for Alured, worse because it was entirely unexpected. He felt that every eye was on him, and wished that he could sink below the carpet. The general went on, speaking as before, with a rapid abbreviating pronunciation, which confused and frightened Alured more than ever.

"Are you in a position, I repeat, to inform me whether you were ever born; and if so, at what ages, and where; whether you were treated after birth, if born at all, with Radway's Ready Relief or Mrs. Winslow's Soothing Syrup, and if so in what quantities, at what intervals? Speak up, young man, and do not keep the court waiting. Can you not answer these questions forthwith?"

"I'm afraid, my lord,—I mean, your excellency,—I cannot at once ——"

"How, young man!" The voice was the deep bass of a theatrical bravo. "You are then lamentably unprepared to assume your new duties. And may I ask whether you have brought a complete kit,—complete in every particular?"

"Yes, I—I hope so, your excellency."

"Yes; you have coat and sword and overall, no doubt; but have you your two pairs of shoe-brushes, your button stick and brush, armourer's forge, three tripods, the requisite number of sandbags, an iron target, a tourniquet, lint and bandages, a pace-stick, pipeclay, and pendulum? You have all these things?"

"No, not exactly,—not all, your excellency."

"How inconceivably careless parents become!" said the general, in a tone of the deepest chagrin, his large, prominent eyes widening till they glared like angry planets as they travelled round the audience. "Have your parents no friends to inform them of the custom and requirements of the service in these matters?"

"My father was in the service himself, your excellency, but some years ago; and ——"

"Then there is no possible excuse: the negligence is the more unpardonable. Captain Davidson, you will see that this young gentleman is provided, from the depot quartermaster's store to-morrow, with the regulation articles of necessaries to complete his kit. That will do, young man. Stay,—would you wish, Brother Jeffries, to put any questions to him?" asked the general, turning to one of the other judges.

"I should like to know how he has been grounded in his military studies. May I ask whether you have learnt the lance exercise, and can take your part without delay in a set of the lancers?"

Alured hung his head.

"You have read the usual authorities—Shuffler, on 'The Evasion of Responsibility,' and Hardbargain on 'Continual Leave'? No? Never heard of them, perhaps? Their principles will be among your acquirements, I can assure you. We know them, most of us, by heart."

"Are you a fast runner?" asked another judge, sharply.

Alured murmured something about school athletics.

"Ay, but have you ever outrun the constable? No? I promise you, you'll find the pace tremendous till you are accustomed to it."

"Mind you don't shirk your work," said the first speaker. "Don't be like 'England.'"

"England?" asked poor Alured in utter amazement.

"'England expects every man to do his duty.' Don't expect any one else to do yours."

"There, there, gentlemen, that will do," interposed the general; "we have much before us. Take Mr. Frere to a seat, Captain Davidson."

Alured was led away dejected and sad at heart. He had never realized that his new profession would be so difficult to follow. Already the glow and glitter was rubbed off, and he half wished himself back at Scaggleton. Davidson, noticing his scared face, introduced him at once to a brandy and soda. Straightway Alured felt lifted off his feet: his heart was lightened, and the clouds disappeared.

Meanwhile the trial proceeded. "*Amicus curiæ*, read the charges," cried the general, in a loud voice, to the gentleman in the black.

"Ensign Christopher Cuthbert, you are here to answer to certain counts and indictments. Are you guilty or not guilty?"

"I must hear them first before I plead."

"Prisoner at the bar, this is contumacy," roared the general; adding *sotto-voce* to his neighbour on the bench, "but there's no bar; get a bar."

"There's none nearer than the canteen," shouted some one.

"Then use a fire-iron."

"*Amicus curiæ*, enter a plea of guilty, and proceed."

"I protest," said Cuthbert.

"Silence! not a word. Go on with the charges."

They were as follows :—

"1st. Conduct unbecoming, and to the prejudice of good order and military discipline, in having joined without a bath-tub.

"2nd. Disobedience of orders in having failed to provide himself with the aforesaid article, at the shop of Mr. Patrick Cassidy, at Ballybanagher.

"3rd. Mutiny and insubordination in the following instances :—

"First instance. In having brought with his kit two suits of respectable black.

"Second instance. In neglecting to be measured for a suit of grey dittoes at the depot tailor's shop.

"Such conduct being calculated to aggravate his brother officers and bring discredit on the depot master tailor."

Witnesses were then called.

One Ensign Fitz-Herbert Smith deposed to having seen the prisoner's baggage entering the barrack square upon a wagon. There were several packages, but no bath-tub; that he could see. He mentioned it at the time to Mr. Gregson.

Cross-examined by the prisoner. "Do you know a bath-tub when you see it?"

"I do."

"Have you one of your own?"

The general interposed, and said the question could not be put.

Lieutenant Gregson was called. He had been with Mr. Smith, and had been surprised to see no tub among the prisoner's baggage when it arrived. Thought it so odd that he took the first opportunity of visiting the prisoner's quarters. There was no tub in the passage.

Cross-examined. "Did you look in my room?"

A. "I did not."

Q. "Might I not have kept the tub in my room?"

A. "No one does."

The general thought this was quite conclusive.

The third witness was Ensign Hewson Dalrymple. He was on intimate terms with the prisoner. Had joined at the same time—they were at drill together—witness was generally late for early parade—prisoner never was. Witness could only account for it by supposing the prisoner did not "tub."

Assistant-Surgeon Mogford, fourth witness, stated that according to custom he had inspected the prisoner's kit on arrival. It was customary to make this inspection in order to allot the new neck-ties and the coloured shirts fairly among the other officers. Nothing worth annexing had been found in the prisoner's boxes; but the black suits now produced in court (their production gave rise to the most marked agitation on the prisoner) had been discovered and tried on—they were found quite unsuited for wear in Ballybanagher. Witness reported the matter.

Cross-examined. "Are you in the habit of inspecting the boxes of newly joined officers."

A. "I sometimes do."

Q. "Have you never been accused of stealing?"

A. "Never."

"Ah," said the prisoner, "then you will be."

Brevet-Major Birch was then called into court and examined by the prosecutor.

Q. "You have been some years in the service?"

A. "Twenty-two."

Q. "And have had much experience of barrack life?"

A. "I have lived in quarters all that time."

Q. "What do you know about the charge?"

A. "Hearing rumours that the prisoner did not tub, I felt it my duty, in the interests of discipline, to make a domiciliary visit to his quarters. I could find no bath-tub, either in the room or in the passage. I examined the floor carefully, there was no trace of damp such as is invariably deposited by the outer periphery of the tub. My suspicions thus aroused, I paid a second visit, at an earlier hour of the morning just after the prisoner had risen. He had clearly not used his tub."

Cross-examined. "You state that you visited my room early in the morning."

A. "Yes; at about 6.30 a.m."

Q. "How were you dressed?"

The *amicus curiæ* objected.

The prisoner urged that the question was most important, and the general permitted it.

Q. "How were you dressed? In a red jacket?"

A. "I was."

Q. "And white waistcoat?"

A. "And white waistcoat."

Q. "In 'mess-dress' in fact?"

A. "Not to put too fine a point upon it, in mess-dress."

Q. "This was at 6.30 a.m. Do you usually put on mess-dress, that is to say evening dress, when you get up of a morning?"

A. "Never."

Q. "And you do not sleep in it, I presume?"

A. "Certainly not."

Q. "Then how came you to be in that dress, at 6.30 a.m.?"

A. "I was returning from mess."

Q. "In other words you had been up all night?"

A. "Well—I had."

Q. "Now can you swear that you didn't see two bath-tubs, instead of none? Will you swear that you were ever in my room at all? Are you certain it was not your own room, which is opposite mine?"

Here the general interposed, declaring that the cross-examination was irrelevant and must cease. The prisoner bowed to the decision of the court, but hoped he might be allowed to put a few questions on another point. This was conceded.

Q. "Were you at mess on the occasion of the last general inspection?"

A. "I was. But I am at a loss to conceive how that——"

Q. "Wait,—you sat up late?"

A. "Till the general left, about 2 a.m."

Q. "And then went to your own quarters to bed?"

A. " Yes, to bed."

Q. " Will you swear that you slept in your own bed ?"

A. " Well——"

Q. " Have you a large iron coal-box in your room ?"

A. " I have."

Q. " Six feet by four ?"

A. " I never measured it."

Q. " Full of coals ?"

A. " Always."

Q. " Do you generally sleep in it ?"

A. " Of course not."

Q. " Will you swear you were not found there the morning after that dinner, or that your clothes were not in the fire-place, or that your bed was not full of coals ?"

The witness became covered with confusion, and appealed to the court for protection. The general got up in wrath. " This is without exception the most unprecedented—" he began, when a man rushed in, breathless, and whispered a few words in the great man's ear.

" The enemy on the move ? Is it so ? Ha! In which direction ?"

"Ballaborris."

"The outposts must be strengthened and that speedily. Which of you is acquainted with the *locale* of Ballaborris?"

Frere stepped forward, surprised at his own boldness, but he owed it to a second brandy and soda, and said that he had come that night from Ballaborris, and would gladly show the way.

"*Euge puer!* You promise well. You shall accompany the reinforcement. Come, let us be moving."

And with that the general rose to his feet, and seemed, possibly from emotion, to be rather unsteady in his gait. Alured was hustled out rather sharply, but not before he had seen Davidson slap the great man on the back, saying, "Hold up, admiral, old chap." Why admiral and not general? Was it simply a mistake of Davidson's? Outside the night was dark as pitch; a drizzling rain had set in; the ground was deep in slush and mud. Enough to damp the ardour of Alured's conductors, but at the foot of the mess-house steps they met a man enveloped in a large military cloak, and accompanied by a sergeant with a lantern. They hailed him.

"What, McLoughlin? Going your rounds?"

The new comer growled out an affirmative. Then some short sentences passed, and Alured caught, "It's such a night." "But he's so keen, we mustn't baulk him," with a murmur or two of suppressed laughter.

"Come, Mr. Frere," said the man in the cloak, who was introduced as Captain McLoughlin; "the troops are marching by the high-road; we will cut across."

The others returned to the mess, but Alured went on with McLoughlin, convinced for the moment that he was about to take part in an important and solemn incident of real warfare. A pretty dance they led him. Through the wet fields, and by slushy lanes, or solitary paths, summoned at intervals to halt and give the countersign, while bayonets glittered in the scant light of the lantern, arms rattled, and short sharp words of command were scattered about like hailstones. Alured remarked innocently that he had no notion the country was in such a state. "They know nothing in England," McLoughlin said;

"the fact was Government was afraid to make it public. But it kept them all constantly on the alert at Ballybanagher." "Who were the enemy?" Alured asked, "insurgents?" "Blue boys," McLoughlin told him vaguely, "and all that;" debating at the same time whether he should not throw in Prince Menschikoff with a few squadrons of Cossacks. Alured swallowed it all greedily, and kept on with a manful stride, though terribly weary long before the rounds were at an end. Presently they reached the town of Ballybanagher, itself one long street of miserable houses, all dark, silent, and seemingly deserted. McLoughlin was making for the one solitary inn, Corrigan's, which adorned the place, meaning to take a car and drive back to barracks, when a yell, clear-drawn and distinct, cut through the stillness like a knife. It was followed by another and another, and by a confused hubbub of voices. Then rapid footfalls neared them, dropping thud, thud, thud, with measured cadence as of men coming along at a swinging trot. "It's the picquet," said McLoughlin's sergeant. "There's fighting, sir, I'll go warrant, at Tim Hogan's."

"Oh, let's go too," cried Alured, forgetting in his ardour that he was fatigued. "We may be of use." McLoughlin did not explain that Tim Hogan's was a whisky shop, haunted by absentees from barracks, subject to nightly rows and under the ban of the police; but leaving Alured to imagine he was about to take part in an affair with the enemy, pressed on, side by side with the picquet. They reached Tim Hogan's. The door went in like paper before them. Alured was one of the first up the narrow stairs, though the sergeant vainly sought to restrain him. A new and thrilling sight for such a raw recruit! The room was long, low, and badly lighted, filled with a mob of people, hideous with the crash of voices, angry and incessant; belts off, shillelaghs playing, women tearing at their favourite men to hold them back from the fray.

Alured dashed into the thick of it. He was in plain clothes, and his own side did not know him. In a second a swinging pipeclay belt, wielded by a powerful soldier in his shirt sleeves, stretched him senseless on the floor.

CHAPTER VII.

LIFE AT THE DEPOT.

Justice Shallow.—There was I; and little John Doit of Staffordshire, and black George Bare, and Francis Pickbone, a Cotswold man. . . . There was Jack Falstaff, now Sir John, a boy and a page to Thomas Mowbray, Duke of Norfolk. . . .

Oh the mad days that I have spent! And to see how many of my acquaintances are dead.

King Henry IV. Part Second.

WHEN Alured came to himself it was broad daylight. Mogford, the young doctor whom he had seen the night before at the trial, stood by his bedside, asking him how he felt.

"Queerish, eh? Don't wonder at it. Here, take this 'pick-me-up.' It'll put you straight in no time."

Alured was most anxious to know what had happened, and where he was.

"You got a cracker on the head last night, that's all. Mac brought you home in a car, and we put you to bed. These are Davidson's quarters."

"What time is it?"

"Past twelve."

"So late. May I get up?"

"Of course—if you're equal to it. Davidson's servant's outside. He'll get your tub and things ready. Come over to the mess when you're dressed."

The servant said Davidson was away in the drill-field, but he'd be back soon on his way to breakfast, and presently the captain came in.

"All right this morning? It was a shame of us to send you out that way."

Alured was still somewhat bewildered, and longed to ask all about the events of the previous night. But Davidson rather evaded the subject.

"Hungry are you? Then you can't be much wrong. Come along; I've ordered breakfast."

It was the same room that had served as court-house. A long table ran down the centre, at which a dozen or more men were seated, nearly all of whom looked up and smiled pleasantly on Alured as he came in.

"Good morning, Frere."

"Good morning."

"Hope you're all right?"

"None the worse?"

"Poor joke for you, after all," and so forth, leading Alured to understand that he had become a sort of centre for their sympathies.

"Where's the admiral? Not been over yet?" asked some one.

"He's late."

"A lot of recruits have come in; they're keeping him at the hospital."

"There's his voice."

It was the same deep bass that Alured had heard presiding at the trial. The "general" and old Draycott, the adjutant, came in together. They were both laughing hugely at some story, and Draycott was saying,—"You know you mustn't do it. There'll be another row. The general,—the real chap I mean—"

Alured looked up, and caught the mock general's eye.

"Halloa, small chap!" roared the general or the admiral, or Starkie, surgeon in charge, as I shall call him in future, "you're there are you? How do you feel this morning?

None the worse I hope. Not a bad beginning for such an infant. They say you performed prodigies of valour. But don't go on this way, or we must send you back to your mother; if we're not all lagged for infanticide."

"Don't mind him, Frere," said Davidson, good-naturedly. "His sense of repartee is blunted, is the admiral's, of a morning. His jokes are too feeble."

"I thought he was a general?"

"And he's only a doctor after all!" roared Starkie, with a great guffaw. Then, changing his tone, he summoned the waiter.

"Mess-waiter, bring me a glass of water."

"Yes, sir," going.

"And, mess-waiter,—put a little brandy in it."

"Yes, sir," going again.

"And,—mess-waiter, you can leave out the water."

A strange being, this Starkie; one of the last of the hard-drinking men of a by-gone generation, who, thanks to an iron constitution, had survived his fellows, and stood like a bit of drift timber left by the receding tide just above water-mark,—a tall, handsome man, with something still of the old rollicking devil-may-care address which had won him once success among a certain class, and made him piquant and interesting even now to the young men at Ballybanagher. See him of an evening, late, as he leant with half-drunken solemnity against the mantelpiece, with a brandy and soda in one hand, while he waved the other to and fro as he gesticulated and laid down the law to the youngsters standing open-mouthed around. To bed in the small hours; but no matter at what hour he turned in, half-past eight next morning saw him at his hospital, and woe to assistant or sergeant who was not there to receive him. Towards noon he came back to mess, and made a giant's breakfast. While thus employed, you might hear the deep tones of his tremendous voice abusing the mess-waiters, or entertaining a select audience with questionable stories. Such was old Starkie,—"the admiral," as they called him aptly enough, from his high and mighty "quarter-deck" manner, from the long stride with which he paced the ante-room, and from his big speaking-trumpet tones, as if he were continually hailing the captain of the main-top. A kind-hearted man withal, who would sit up night after night to watch the bedside of man, woman, or child who needed it; refusing drink the while till he brought himself by his abstinence on the verge of delirium tremens. A man of varied experience, and well up in the work of his own profession, but a dangerous companion for the wild lads at Ballybanagher.

Such a team of unmanageable colts no Jehu had ever been called upon to drive. Some but just emancipated from school and home restraints, were still half-mad with excitement; others, a few months older, had already tasted of the knowledge of the world, but in those small doses which are proverbially dangerous. The latter took the lead at Ballybanagher; there was no one to keep them in check. The colonel commanding, his major and adjutant, were married, and lived away from mess; of the few captains present, some were either children like the rest, prematurely promoted, or aged broken-down men like Birch, who had no influence whatever. So Starkie and half a dozen choice spirits, self selected, ruled the roast. According to their verdict, the newly joined ensign was treated well or ill. In those days vacancies were so numerous, and the demand for new officers so great, that the new comers were rather a mixed lot. Old and young, rich and poor, gentleman and cad. One aged ensign brought his wife and children to watch from their barrack room poor papa performing painful exercises in the drill-field. Bulger was another specimen; a snob so atrocious that it was a mystery how he had passed muster at the Horse Guards. Starkie declared that he was put into the army by Skylarkers, the great contractors, as "tout" for their establishment. Bulger's antecedents were unmistakeably commercial. He checked his mess and wine account by double entry, and kept a petty cash book to record his daily expenditure. St. Pierre, again, was of a different stamp. Educated in France, he spoke English like a foreigner, and could "do" nothing except argue: neither shoot, fish, ride or play at cricket,—deficiencies sadly in his disfavour, and receiving a greater prominence from his worship of French institutions, from his outspoken contempt for "you English," and his readiness to maintain all day and every day the case Bonaparte *versus* Wellington. With such men as these Starkie's committee made short work. "Frenchy" found his door nailed up most nights when he got back from mess, or the ends of his trousers sewn across next morning, so that he was late for early parade. They pitchforked Bulger's furniture out of the window, and cobbed him when he talked about assessed damages. For poor Annandale, the aged ensign, who was rather short-sighted, they laid traps in the mess-room; thin lines of gut, as strong as steel, extending between the joints on the sideboard and the legs of the ponderous mess-room table, across which he stumbled and fell, bringing dishes and all to the ground. Bloxam, better known in after-life as "Barnacle Bloxam," from the tenacity with which he held on to the great people he floated against, was treated with more leniency, because, even in that early stage of this his limpet-life existence, he attached himself to Starkie's committee as representing something superior to himself: he gave them champagne grog-fights in his room, and stood a drag and lunch all round for Knockalofty Races. Bloxam must have been descended from the peculiar people, so sumptuous were his tastes. His quarters, furnished as he thought with unparalleled splendour, were like a back parlour in Wardour Street: all costly engravings, silk velvet, gilt chairs, mirrors, and bricabrac. Cassidy, the general dealer in Ballybanagher, did it all for him. In this tasteful boudoir he passed his spare hours lounging negligently on a sofa, in a crimson brocaded dressing-gown, with an embroidered smoking-cap upon his nicely oiled locks; reading, at least holding in his hand, a handsomely bound book, but the contents were of less consequence than its gilded edges and morocco cover. It was a sight, too, to see him issue forth dressed to captivate the neighbouring natives. His long great coat had to be lifted at a muddy crossing,—and Ballybanagher itself was one long crossing,—like a lady's skirt; his umbrella was barely as big as a toothpick; his trousers fell like an extinguisher over his brilliant shoes, hiding, except at rare intervals, the flashes of his rainbow-hued socks and gorgeous bows. Other young men there were at Ballybanagher whose peculiarities were not less strongly marked. Some went in wildly for athletics. Clayton climbed daily from window to window, till he reached the roof. Parkins made wagers that he would walk to Knockalofty and back, eighteen miles, in five hours. Trowbridge's dreams were of dogs; rats were his only aim. Ainstie joined with a strongly-developed taste for entomology, and after enduring much persecution, and the titles of Crusher or Beetle Ainstie, founded a school of his own. But he and his followers were the adjutant's especial aversion. Even in the drill-field, science absorbed them, and intricate manœuvres failed because an actor here and there had stooped to pick up an insect. Billiards claimed the worship of many. The green-table at Corrigan's hotel witnessed more than one discreditable fracas: scuffles with billiard cues, doubtful play, and bets mismanaged. Nor were these the only scrapes into which the young men fell. Gambling at sixpenny loo, heavy nights at mess, and so forth. There is always work of a certain kind for idle hands; and it was too much to expect old heads upon all these young shoulders.

Alured might have fared badly at first in this motley crew. For his youth and innocence had marked him down as an easy prey the very night of his arrival. But there had been a strong reaction in his favour after the pluck he displayed in the shebeen house brawl. He had stoutly resisted moreover all attempts on the part of the adjutant to elicit the particulars of the row; an immense let-off for McLoughlin, Davidson, and others, who dreaded the consequences of an *exposé*. An officer struck by a private soldier in a pot-house, has an ugly sound, reader. It means a general court-martial, with all sorts of pains and penalties for those concerned. So the young fellows were most grateful for his reticence. But Draycott did not like it. He was a busybody with a conscience, who felt it his duty to ferret out everything, for the colonel's private ear. Now Alured, as a recruit, was handed over to the adjutant, body and soul, and Draycott could not forget all at once that he had been baffled. At the first drill parade he was more than usually grumpy. Alured had come out flushed with excusable pride, in all the glory of a scarlet jacket indued for the first time. Draycott, looking at him from head to foot, addressed him with a sneer, thus :—

"And what do you expect me to do with you? You're too small to hold a rifle; and I can't put you in front of a squad of recruits, they'd laugh at you. You'd better go and play with the other children there," pointing to a group of soldiers' brats, busy at mud-pies in a distant corner of the square.

Alured, wounded to the heart, stepped out and began to stammer " he was past sixteen."

"Silence, sir!" roared the adjutant, monarch irresponsible and implacable. " Don't answer *me*, sir. Don't speak in the ranks, sir. You've got to learn a lot, and that's one of the first lessons. Fall in!"

A hot flush sprang to Alured's cheek. He had yet to learn indifference—stolid indifference—to the abrupt peremptoriness that comes to be a second nature with those who command soldiers, and are commanded by them.

His fellow-ensigns, when the drill was over told him not to mind old Draycott. He was a brute always. But not the less did Alured chafe at Draycott's treatment on this and subsequent occasions. Why should the adjutant single out him, and him only, for constant attack? Was he, Frere, the only one who was always wrong —who moved off always with right foot instead of left (as if it mattered!); who forgot which was the "front," and hesitated about "changing his flank" at the word of command? His earliest letters home,—and hither he turned, not unnaturally, to pour out his woes and gather sympathy,—were tinged with the unhappiness he felt. In reply, the major laughed at him, pointing his jests with wise soldier saws that might have made copybook headings in a military school. "The adjutant is the recruits' best friend;" "Silent suffering is the backbone of discipline;" "Insubordination is the ruin of armies;" and so forth. Brave-hearted Mrs. Frere understood him better, and, knowing the medicine he needed, wrote encouraging words, bidding him face his troubles and beat them. It was early in the fight, she said, to succumb. The adjutant was a hateful man, but perhaps he acted for the best. A mother's sympathy goes straight home to the heart at Alured's age. He began to pluck up his courage remembering how some such assistance from the same loving source had tided him over τυπτω into the deepest Greek. Surely the drill-book was not tougher than Thucydides; to form square on the two centre subdivisions must be child's play to iambics. Davidson helped him, and McLoughlin; he read and pondered day after day, till the diagrams ceased to bewilder him, and he had grasped in his memory the parrot-like utterances that constitute the words of command. With knowledge came confidence. He found that he could stand unabashed before a company of men, even with Draycott at his elbow. The lad was so anxious, and took such evident pains to succeed, that in the end he won a complete victory over his cruel task-master. Draycott relented, and began to love the lad in his own surly fashion; patting him on the back with such approving speeches as "You'll do yet, Boy Frere;" "I've made a man of you;" and "I wish there were more like you."

Other trials, more difficult to overcome than drill, met him at this the onset of his career. Temptations thickly strew the path of youth just emancipated. But Alured was firmly fixed in the principles he had learned at home. He could not condescend to gamble, drink, or swear, as many around him did, even in a moderate degree. His mind, pure, and still uncontaminated, shrank with sensitive shyness from Starkie's double-edged stories; and those with whom he lived respected his innocence, admiring his inoffensive blameless life. After a month at Ballybanagher, there was no one more universally popular than "Boy Frere."

CHAPTER VIII.

MOYNEHAN CASTLE; ON THE THRESHOLD.

" There was a sound of revelry by night,
 . . . and bright
The lamps shone o'er fair women and brave men."
Childe Harold.

"You're in luck, Frere."

"How so?"

It was breakfast-time, and a dozen or more officers were in the mess-room, some at table, others turning over on the mantelpiece the letters lying there that had arrived by that morning's post. Alured had just come in, and he repeated his question.

"Why am I in luck?"

"Here's a ticket for you. You're the only man they've asked!"

"Man! do you call that thing a man? He's a child, and it's a children's party; that's why they want him."

"You'll have to play with Miss What's-her-name; and you'll have tea and jam in the nursery; and we'll send the maid for you at eight punctually."

"But where am I asked? For goodness' sake tell me!"

"For goodness' sake! How nicely he swears! You're coming on. It'll be something much stronger soon," said old Birch.

"Give him the card," interposed Davidson, who had just come in.

"If I don't let him have it, he can't go. Do you want to go very much, boy?"

"Boy yourself! But go where? Give it me, do," cried Alured rather pettishly, stretching across the table.

"Hands off! None of your snatching, Boy Frere."

"If you're so rough, they won't ask you to the Castle any more," said some one else. "You'll be hurting the other children."

"The Castle?"

"Yes, the Castle; fancy that," continued his tormentor. "Here, look. Can you read it across the table? The letters are big enough, I'm sure. Listen—

"'The Countess of Moynehan will be at home to Mr. Frere of the 145th, on the 13th at 9 o'clock;' and there's to be dancing and divilments of all kinds, I don't doubt."

Alured remembered Moynehan Castle well enough. It was the home of that queenly personage who had pitied and petted him when so forlorn.

"What do you mean by it, Boy Frere?" asked Davidson laughingly, as he took the card, and gave it to Alured. "What do you mean by coming down here with your sham innocence and childish ways, when it turns out you are hand and glove with all the lords and ladies in the place? Here have we been all of us ten months or more at Ballybanagher, and never has a man of us darkened old Moynehan's doors."

The fact was the neighbouring county families looked with little favour on the overgrown depot which occupied the barracks, and did not care to make acquaintances.

"Here's Bloxam," went on Davidson, "ready to pay handsomely for a ticket like that, just to frame it, and hang it over his mantelpiece.

And you, you miserable little beggar, are asked to a dance at the Castle within a month or two of your joining. What do you mean by it, eh?"

"Come on; I'm not afraid of you," cried Alured, squaring up to his captain. "I'll fight you for the invitation."

"You've lots of cheek, you have. It was only yesterday, about, that you called me Sir, and seemed so soft that butter wouldn't melt in your mouth. Now, you're offering to strike your superior officer. Do you know it is a court-martial offence?"

"Oh, yes; I know all about your courts-martial. Give me the card,—will you, or won't you?"

"Well—I will. There, boy, take it, and gladden your eyes with it. But don't get snobbish, and gloat over the big names too much. These fellows are dying with envy at your luck; but don't think too much of it, I tell you. You'll wish yourself back here, when once you get to the Castle."

"I won't. Why should I?"

"Because the people you meet at those places

have a way of looking at you till you begin to feel like an escaped criminal or a lost dog—quite out of place, and liable to instant capture and removal."

Bloxam had been deep in thought for some time. At last he remarked speculatively, "I wonder how you managed to get this ticket, Frere? They tell me the countess is a real knock-me-down fine lady."

"Who never speaks to anything under a duke," shouted Starkie, "and has baronets for footmen, eh?"

"No, but—"

"You wonder why Boy Frere is asked? Perhaps they'll invite you too, if you dress yourself in a suit of sky blue velvet, and drive up and down in front of the lodge."

"You're always down on me, Starkie. You know I haven't got a suit of blue velvet."

Everybody grinned.

"I met Lord and Lady Moynehan at Ballaborris station, and they gave me a seat as far as this in their carriage," said Frere, apologetically almost, to the whole company.

"And as you didn't pick his lordship's

pockets, or tread upon her ladyship's toes, they wish to keep up the acquaintance. Natural enough," said Davidson.

Bloxam said nothing, but he came to the conclusion that introduction was everything. Perhaps if the Moynehans were to meet him too, they might give him the *entrée* to their house. When he returned to his quarters, he searched his wardrobe—not for sky blue velvet, but for something striking, in which he might parade himself for the inspection of the countess the next time the band played on the mall at Ballybanagher.

When the night of the 13th arrived, Alured, in fear and trembling, arrayed himself in a tail coat, and tied, for the first time in his life, a white cravat around his neck. For Alured Frere, ætat sixteen years and two months, had never been to an evening party before, still less to a ball at an earl's castle. His luck in being the only officer invited reacted rather on himself. He had to travel to Moynehan alone, five dreary miles, with no company but his own thoughts. As he got nearer and nearer to the scene of this new ordeal, his courage sank, and threatened soon to evaporate altogether. Despair was in his heart when, passing the lodge gates and entering the drive, he knew that his hour had come. Not far from the house, Alured's car joined itself to a string of carriages moving slowly forward to where a great stream of blazing light issued forth from the entrance hall. In this bright white ray the wet holly bushes glistened and twinkled; footmen in long drab coats came and went; here and there was the sparkle of gold or brilliants, and figures in fluffy gauze or transparent tulle floated by like clouds swift on the wing. Poor little Alured was quite bewildered when it came to his turn to descend from the Irish car where he sat perched, and he entered abashed and humble in the full gaze of the liveried lackeys who stood around, calmly superior and indifferent. None of them offered to take his coat or hat, nor did any servant address him, but one led the way to a grand staircase, and reaching the first of a suite of antechambers, gave a superb wave of his hand, as much as to say—" There you are; it's all before you." A long vista of rooms, empty most of them, but Alured could see an occasional pair of calves ranging away in the distance, the property of other retainers placed like buoys to mark the passage. Alured walked on in silent awe, and with a cold feeling at his heart that he had come the wrong night. Why had he not brought the card with him? or was he too late, or too early? By degrees he got into the channel, drifting past couples together in corners, or an old gentleman buttonholed by another old gentleman. Then the shipping, to continue our metaphor, became more numerous; crafts of every build and rig, under full sail, or lying at anchor, and presently he reached the haven itself, the ball-room, crammed full of people. Round about the doorway was a dense hedge of heads, but between the interstices, a glimpse was caught of flying figures within, careering wildly to the tune of a furiously rapid waltz.

As yet, no one had come forward to receive Alured, and he felt rather uncomfortable. Everybody but himself seemed to know other people; he alone had not a friend to throw him a civil word. Already he began to remember Davidson's prophecy that he would wish himself home again. To retrace his steps, and run for it was his first impulse; but, like Cortes, he had burned his ships, by sending away his car, and his line of retreat was closed till two in the morning.

Soon the music stopped, and the couples that had been dancing came out past him. He imagined that they were all staring at him. One old dowager drove him nearly frantic by inspecting him closely through her eye-glass.

Was there anything wrong with his dress? He looked at the other men, and noted the style of their neck-ties, the cut of their coats, and seemed to see a difference. It is not unusual for people—young men, shy boys, and women, particularly—to be affected by the style or condition of their apparel. Dress has often a potent influence upon their actions and their peace of mind. A man must be either very self-possessed or very simple-minded who can continue to speak impressively to a large audience, when the bow of his neck-tie has got close under his left ear. There are some angelic females who can continue to be charming even when they know their bonnets to be crooked or their hair is tumbling down their backs. But these are surely the exceptions. The sense of misfit, of inappropriateness of the appearance in a high dress, when everybody else is in a low, in a frock coat instead of a swallow-tail—this external inconformity checks, as a rule, all buoyancy of spirit, ruins the temper, ties the tongue. So Alured thought, painfully, that of the other men he saw about, some had on white waistcoats, some had velvet collars to their coats, and some had brought their hats upstairs. Feeling more uncomfortable every moment, he tried to sneak off and hide in some out-of-the-way corner. But there was no loophole of escape, that he could see.

At that moment he would have gladly hired at a high price a partner just to escort him across the passage and round the corner. But no charming girl was likely to offer herself, even as a temporary loan.

Then said some one *en passant*—

"I cannot understand why the Moynehans fill their rooms with such a set. Did you ever see such odd people?"

It is a guest's privilege, of course, to find fault with his host,—to abuse his bread while he eats it, and pick holes in his companions. A very general practice, perhaps, but new to Alured, who took the ill-natured remark entirely to himself. Rather than listen to such criticisms, he turned tail and fled.

Fled past ottoman and couch, through a picture gallery, a card-room, and a library, till he reached a retired spot,—a couple of small rooms, seemingly the thoroughfare to another part or wing of the castle, fitted up with simple furniture but very snug and quiet, and unassuming. Here, in a wide arm-chair before the fire, Alured ensconced himself, taking first a book from the shelves at hand. But Hallam's History of Literature could not absorb his attention altogether. He found himself debating whether it was possible for him to escape from the house. He had quite enough of the ball already. But how to face the men at Ballybanagher to-morrow? At this moment a voice close by roused him from his thoughts and Hallam's History. A new voice to him, but sweet and clear as a silver chime—

"Why don't you go and dance?"

The question was repeated before Alured answered, and the second time there was a pretty petulance in the query.

He looked up, and saw before him a child; though, after all, she was only a few years younger than himself. A pretty, *petite*, fairy-like creature, with great, wide-open, astonished brown eyes, and a torrent of soft black hair hurrying down below her waist in rippling tresses. She tapped her little shoe on the floor again and again, as she cried—

"Why don't you go and dance, I say?"

"I can't dance. I don't know how."

"Not dance? Not waltz or galop? Why I can't remember when I couldn't dance. But—"

She was doubting whether he was really a guest, or whether it was right for her to be speaking to him. It was not usual, she thought, for gentlemen to say they couldn't dance.

"Are you—?" She wanted to ask him who he was, but could not frame the question rightly.

"I am an officer. From the barracks at Ballybanagher."

"An officer! How nice! But where's your red coat? Don't you officers wear red coats? and swords? and sashes? I've seen them often. But "—again doubts assailed her—" I don't believe you are an officer. You're too—"

"Too what?"

"Too young."

Alured laughed. "I'm older than you are, I dare say."

"I dare say. But I'm not an officer."

"Would you like to be?"

A very decisive negative shake of the head.

"Not a bit." Then, "But why don't you go into the ballroom? Do you know many people?"

"You're the first person I have spoken to to-night, and no one has spoken to me."

"What, hasn't aunt? Haven't you made your bow to my aunt? Nor to Uncle Moynehan? Shall we go and see them? Don't you know them?"

"I met them once at Ballaborris station, and

they took me to the barracks in their carriage."

"Why you must be the little officer that aunt said would just do to play with me. Play with me, indeed! But, I say, wasn't it funny we should meet in this way?"

"I'm delighted."

"Thank you. But I was told I wasn't to come down to the ball. Then I heard music, and oh, it was so stupid in the schoolroom; so I made Hedger—that's our maid, you know—dress me, and here I am."

"And very nice you look."

"Yes; don't I!" said she. "But do let us go in and dance. Stay; I forgot you couldn't dance. Never mind; we'll stop here. If I did go into the ballroom, I should be ordered straight off to bed. We'll stay and talk here, —that is, if you don't mind."

"Oh no; I don't mind," replied Alured, highly amused.

"And I'll tell you what we'll do; we will sit out like two grown-up people and flirt. Do you know how to flirt?" she added, looking at him with her great innocent eyes.

"Not in the least. You shall teach me."

"Very well. Sit down there,—not so far off. Now look in my face, and say something."

"What sort of thing?"

"Oh, something interesting, amusing, pleasant."

Alured could not for the life of him imagine what to say.

"Can't you begin? Can you say nothing?"

"I never felt so stupid in all my life."

"We can't go on like this, you know. People would think it so odd. Shall I show you some pictures, or my flowers in the conservatory. No; the conservatory is too far off; but we've got a famous quantity of hothouse plants here close by. Come, come along; don't be afraid," said the little lady, with a patronising pat of the hand.

She led the way into the next room, at the far end of which, behind a heavy curtain, was a sort of winter garden on a balcony apparently closed in with glass.

"And you haven't got a flower in your button-hole! Well! I declare I have never seen any one in this house without a flower in his button-hole. Have this camelia, will you?"

"Are you sure you may pick it?"

"Oh, yes. But I must cut it. Wait only a minute; I'll run for a pair of scissors."

She was off like an arrow from a bow.

Alured waited patiently where he was; but the seconds flew by, and he began to wonder what kept her. He was on the point of following the little maid, when voices approaching cautioned him to remain concealed.

"Here; come in here."

It was Lady Moynehan herself who swept into the room, accompanied by a servant in livery.

"What are you doing in this house? How dare you come here? What is the meaning of this dress?"

"It means, my lady, that I am now footman to Sir Arthur Gore, and I am helping in the supper-room."

He was in plush, silk stockings, and powder, with square-cut whiskers; in every respect a strictly correct "Jeames."

"What brought you to these parts?"

"I only came to see her."

"*Her!* Whom?"

"Millicent. I must see her."

"She is in bed, hours ago."

"Excuse me, I saw her run from this room, not a minute ago. I *must* see her, and hear her voice again."

Millicent at this moment ran in.

"Millicent!" cried her ladyship, in a vexed tone; "what are you doing, up and dressed at this time of night? You ought to have been in bed hours ago. Run away, my child, and tell Hedger she was wrong to let you come."

Millicent went off with a slow, lingering step, hanging her head, but without a word.

When she was out of sight, Lady Moynehan turned to her companion. "Now, you will be good enough to go too."

The man scowled, and said with an oath, "Do not provoke me."

"Is this the way you keep your promises? Unless you leave my house this instant, I'll have you turned out. I must see whether I cannot teach you to keep your place. Perhaps

I may, through your pocket. I will stop the payment I have made hitherto, unless you engage to leave this neighbourhood at once. But I wonder at your effrontery at entering this house. Begone, I say, or I will have you turned out."

"You daren't, my lady."

The man had recovered himself, and with native impudence began to swagger. There was evidently some secret between them—a disagreeable secret; for as he waxed more rude and menacing, she became strangely agitated, though striving to look and speak bravely.

"If you raise a cry or lift a finger, my lady, you'll repent it. Do you wish me to announce myself to Lord Moynehan and this houseful of people? Do you want me to tell them who I am? By heavens!" he added, with a brutal laugh, "I'll go and do it now."

"No, no! anything but that."

"I thought that would bring you to book. Be more reasonable."

"What is it you want now? You surely cannot wish to stay in these parts as you are?" pointing to his livery.

"I don't know. It's not a bad crib, Goreham. But I'll go if you particularly wish it."

"Where?"

"Anywhere will suit you, I suppose, if it's only far enough. But you must shell out. I'll collar the swag first. I'll go to the Crimea if you like; there's lots of openings there for honest men."

"What do you require?"

"A couple of monkeys."

"*What?*" Her hesitation was not at the request; but she really did not know what he meant.

"Well, say a hundred."

"In addition?"

"Of course. A bonus as we say in business."

"You shall have it to-morrow."

"No, no, no; none of your gammon. You must pay me here now. I don't budge a foot till I've pouched the dibs. You can't play the fool with me; come, down with the dust."

"Do you suppose I carry hundred pound notes about me sewn up in my ball-dress?

You *must* wait, but you shall have the money I promised you."

" I must have something on account then. I don't trust you women, no not an inch. Here, give me one of those trumpery bracelets. I'll take it as a pledge."

" I cannot, indeed I cannot. You must trust me."

" That I will not. Here, no nonsense," he cried, seizing her wrist roughly.

" Ah!" it was only a little scream, but it brought Alured out from behind the curtain, and the next minute the ruffian was thrown to the ground. There was something in the glowing eye of his young assailant that warned the other when he rose to his feet, that he had better throw up the sponge. 'Almost directly he slunk away and left the room.

Then Lady Moynehan turned at once to Alured, and said to him hurriedly and angrily, " Where did you drop from?"

The reply and conversation which followed deserve another chapter.

CHAPTER IX.

MOYNEHAN CASTLE: GAINING GROUND.

Beatrice advances.
Beat.—What fire is in my ears? Can this be true?
Much Ado about Nothing.

"WHERE did you drop from?" Lady Moynehan had asked while Alured stood like a culprit before her. But not as one hardened in crime, who faces his judge with brazen unabashed front; he hung his head sheepishly, and had not a word to say. But he pointed to the recess in the window.

"How long have you been there? No—tell me first," she went on, rather rudely, "who are you?"

Perhaps this wounded him more than detection. Was he so insignificant and unworthy that within a few weeks she had forgotten him altogether?

"My name is Frere, Alured Frere. You asked me to come to the ball. I'm sure I wish I had not; and I'm very, very sorry."

Of course this was the most cunning method to disarm her anger. In her own heart Lady Moynehan was grateful for his prompt assistance, but she could not forgive him all at once the crime of listening.

"How long were you there, I ask? I mean behind that curtain?"

"Half an hour at least."

"Who, or what took you there?"

"A young lady, I mean a child."

"Millicent!"

"Yes; your niece, I think."

"And did you hear what passed between us—between me and that man? Be honest, Mr. Frere."

Alured looked up into her face, and said as bravely as he could,—

"I'm afraid I heard every word."

"And what do you call yourself—a gentleman? Faugh, I'm surprised at you. What gentleman would listen to other people's conversation?"

"It was hardly my fault, Lady Moynehan. I had no way of escape—except just past you."

"And why did you not take it?" asked her ladyship coldly, and with an incredulous shrug of her white shoulders. The excuse seemed so pitiably inadequate.

"From the first moment I felt that I had heard too much; and I waited hoping—hoping—"

"Yes, hoping—?" she repeated.

"To escape detection altogether." Alured's cheeks grew hotter, and more scarlet. "Pray forgive me, Lady Moynehan, will you—can you? I quite hate myself when I think how meanly I have behaved."

The lad spoke eagerly and fast. He was clearly alive to his fault. Besides there was something so frank and honest in his bright face, that Lady Moynehan read there as in a book that confidence would not be misplaced in Alured Frere.

"Mr. Frere," she spoke very slowly and gravely, "I *will* believe you. I will take you at your word, and will believe that you were an unwilling witness to this humiliating, degrading scene. Oh, if you only knew all—"

It seemed as if a flood of distressing thoughts rushed in upon her. For a time she covered her face in her hands, and turned away.

When she looked up, Alured's eyes met hers. Anguish on one side, tender pity and sympathy on the other.

"Can I trust you, I wonder? You are such a boy."

"Indeed, indeed you may."

"Will you give me your promise,—your word of honour as a gentleman?"

"Only forgive me, Lady Moynehan, and I promise never to breathe a syllable of what has passed to-night."

"I think I may rely upon you. I feel it now. There is my hand upon it."

What could Alured do but take the hand in both his, and dropping to his knees, kiss it glove and all?

Lady Moynehan was not angry with him. Perhaps with a woman's quick perception she understood how much he sought to convey by this *outré* act of worship. But she drew away her hand, and said, almost laughing,—

"Get up, get up, Mr. Frere. It is I, I think,

who should kneel to you, for I am in your power now."

A pause followed, which neither broke till Lady Moynehan said, "I have been away an unconscionable time. Will you give me your arm back to the ballroom, Mr. Frere?"

As they passed out of the little room to the gallery beyond she stopped.

"For the last time, Mr. Frere, repeat your promise. You will not mention this to a single soul?"

"I will not, Lady Moynehan, so help me Heaven."

"I am satisfied."

Very soon this accomplished woman of the world began to talk away with her customary ease. One so well-bred and fashionable had all the arts of pleasing at her finger-ends. And these great dames have the knack of throwing such eager interest in each simple question, the charm of their manner is so fascinating, they show so clearly that all this friendliness is assumed for you and you alone, that most men, I take it, are ready to fall headlong at their feet, and accept as gospel truths every syllable uttered. Lady Moynehan was naturally anxious, after what had happened, to win Alured to her side, and hang him with the chains of pleasant servitude. It was not a very difficult task. Boys always worship women much their seniors.

"You must let me get you some partners," Lady Moynehan said. "There are plenty of nice girls here. But how was it I did not notice you earlier?"

"Perhaps you did not recognise me, Lady Moynehan."

"Perhaps not," she replied, laughing pleasantly. "But don't be angry with me on that account. We have only met once before, and it was very dark then. But I knew your voice to-night. Tell me, when did you arrive? We have such a crowd of people here, you know; it's impossible to shake hands with all directly they come."

They were now quite close to the ballroom, and Alured found courage to falter out,—

"I think I'd rather not dance."

"Not dance? Why? You're too young to be lazy or fine? Oh, you must."

"But I really can't dance."

"Can't. Rubbish, Mr. Frere," cried her ladyship, highly amused. "Come along," and her hand closed quite tightly on his arm.

"I mean I can't dance, because I don't know how."

"Is that all? Well, we must teach you. But," seeing that he still hung back, she added, "I will not worry you if you'd rather not."

"Indeed, I had much rather not."

"As you please. I know you have a will of your own. Do you remember how determined you were that night we dropped you at the barracks? I quite admired you for your strength of mind."

It was very pleasant for him, this sort of flattery. Pleasant to think that she could recollect so well, if she pleased, the last occasion on which they had met. Pleasanter to find there were traits in his character that won from her words of praise. It is thus that a woman of ripe experience and cleverness wins the battle easily over a boy admirer. Descending from her pedestal to pick him up from the crowd, she flatters his pride by praising his good points, and evincing a kindly interest in his welfare.

"And how did you get on that night? You never told me that."

"It's a long story, Lady Moynehan."

"Then it must wait till by-and-by. I will not tax your good nature further now," she said, relinquishing his arm. "We shall meet again before long, I dare say."

She took a few steps, then came back. "You know you owe us a visit. When will you come? Will you stay to-night, and we'll send over for your portmanteau and servant before you are up in the morning?"

He had not got leave; that was his excuse.

"Oh!" she laughed. "I know all about that. You soldiers never have leave, and never can get leave—when you don't choose. But I choose you to have leave this time. I'll write and tell Colonel Willoughby we've kept you. I know him very well. There will be no difficulty."

So it was settled for him. And now, to a certain extent, he had obtained "the freedom of

Moynehan Castle." He was at home, an inmate in the house from which he had longed to escape an hour before.

But though the countess greeted him warmly, she was the only person he knew. The others stared at him just as much as ever; wondering no doubt who he was when they saw him especially favoured by the mistress of the house. Alured wandered from room to room, and by degrees the old feeling of loneliness in a crowd returned to him. He began to regret that he had not made up his mind just to try a quadrille, or if he might only go and talk to Lady Moynehan again. She made herself so pleasant. And was this magnificent personage really in his power? The kindest thing he could do would be to forget what had occurred, —to banish the strange scene from his mind utterly.

Occupied by these thoughts, he wandered about disconsolately, till, long past midnight, he met Lady Moynehan again.

"Why, Mr. Frere, I have been looking for you everywhere. You must not hide in this way, or I shall have to order you to come and speak to me every five minutes, just to prove you're not lost in this great labyrinth of a house. Lord Moynehan wanted to see you; and now I'm afraid he's gone to bed. Late hours don't suit him much. And it's close on supper-time. I want you to take some one in."

"I'm sure I shall be very glad," replied Alured, determined to be more sociable.

"Miss Tremenheere," said Lady Moynehan, to a bright-eyed, round-faced girl, who was sitting alone, "let me introduce my particular friend, Mr. Frere. There, Mr. Frere—now you'll do. Fanny, take care of him!" she added, with a laugh, as she went off.

"Why am I to take care of you?"

"I suppose, because I am not able to take care of myself."

"I should think not, indeed! How came they to let you be out so late at night?"

"Who do you mean by 'they'?"

"Your father, or mother, or tutor, or whoever has the charge of you."

"I'm my own master. I'm an officer in the army, Miss Tremenheere."

"Goodness gracious! do you tell me so! I

thought—" but the merry girl burst into a peal of laughter. "Here, sit down," she said, making room in the corner, by squeezing aside her dress. "You're quite a boy, it's true, but you'll do for me to keep my hand in with."

Alured took the proffered seat, and soon found, by personal inspection, that his companion had beautiful eyes. Blue,—" Irish blue," if I may coin a pigment. Art critics tell us that all colour depends for hue on its juxtaposition with other colours. It is the pink and white flesh, as pure as Parian marble, the ruddy lips, and the beautiful brown hair, that brings out the azure in an Irish girl's eyes. Miss Tremenheere's eyes were as blue and deep as a southern sky at midday.

There is nothing like kindly approval from woman's eyes, to bring a boy up to the mark. They force him, like glass does a cucumber. Alured soon began to have a better opinion of himself, and prattled away without reserve to his new friend. Miss Tremenheere was one of those good-tempered girls, not quite young, but not yet soured by the barren harvests of many succeeding and unsuccessful seasons. She could still find a pleasure in chaffing a boy; although time and metal might have been more profitably employed on a worthier foe.

"You'll do well enough, one of these days," she said, patronizingly.

"When?"

"When you're full-grown—ten years hence."

"That's a long day. I'd like to discount a little."

"What's 'discount' mean?"

"Did you ever hear of the boy that ate his cake and wanted to have it too? If I wait till I'm six-and-twenty, according to you, I shall get my cake; but I want to eat some of it now: That's discount."

"Oh, bother; let's go and discount some supper, and then you shall dance with me. Are you a good mover?"

"I can't dance."

"That's disgraceful. What can you do? Ride?"

"Not much."

"Worse and worse. Shoot?"

"A haystack, perhaps."

"The snipe about here, are not so big as

haystacks, whatever they may be over the water. Flirt?—No; I can answer that."

"How?"

"Well, you have some notion, but vague, very vague. Dear me! how your education has been neglected! I must take you in hand myself. Neither shoot, ride, dance, nor flirt, and you an officer. Oh, Mr. Frere!"

By this time they were in the supper-room discussing soup, champagne, and truffles, at a small table which they had all to themselves. Ambrosial fare, Alured thought, and heavenly company.

"And you don't regret your toffee and hardbake?" asked Miss Tremenheere. "Have you got to like olives, and caviare, and claret, yet? But what's the matter?"

Alured had half started from his chair. Not a dozen yards from him was the scowling face of the man he had seen with Lady Moynehan.

"I thought you wanted something," he said, rather confused.

"Not I; and if I did, it's no reason why you should upset the table."

"Shall we go back to the ballroom?"

"By all means."

They returned, and tried a quadrille, with satisfactory results. Then a set of the lancers: progress less clearly marked, but still satisfactory. After which, Alured suggested himself a fast dance, but Miss Tremenheere would not hear of it yet.

"You're staying in the house are you not, Mr. Frere?"

"For a day or two, I believe."

"Well, then, I'll give you some lessons on the sly, but you'd better not make the experiment for the first time in public. Sara, that's my sister, and Bob,—we're to be here for a week."

"Who's Bob?"

"My brother. Don't you know Bob? Everybody knows Bob. He's in the Halberdiers. I'll introduce you. I'm sure you'll like him."

"I shall, if—"

"If what?"

"If he's as nice as the rest of the family," blurted out Alured.

"Bravo, Mr. Frere! I thought you'd get on. But let me tell you, it's not usual to pay such broad compliments. Some people call it bad taste."

By the time the ball was over, Alured was on excellent terms with his new friend. And not with her alone. Other girls received him well, and allowed him to dance with them; and the great "Bob" had promised him protection.

It was very late when Alured got to bed, The pale winter's dawn was trying to steal in through the window-curtains, but it was not strong enough to overcome the blazing firelight or the wax candles on the dressing-table. Although Alured's servant could not be expected till the morning, there were preparations for his comfort. Brushes, ivory-backed, nightshirt, even a dressing-gown and slippers. They didn't do things by halves at Moynehan. Such a jolly room too! not too big to be snug. Pretty chintz hangings, a bright carpet; on the walls a few curious old prints in black and gold frames. There was a smell of lavender in the sheets, and of dried flowers and sandal wood in the walnut wardrobe.

The other men had gone off to smoke, but Alured prepared to turn in at once. The fact was, he had not learned to smoke yet. There were so many things, as Miss Tremenheere told him, which he had yet to learn. But knowledge of the kind he lacked would come soon enough, unsought. The world has much to teach, lessons both good and bad, and its pupils cannot quite choose their own curriculum. A man who has got his experience by heart, has indeed, tasted of the tree of knowledge, and knows both good and evil.

That night at Moynehan, our hero had barely got his teeth into the fruit.

CHAPTER X.

MOYNEHAN CASTLE: QUITE AT HOME.

> "Poor boy," she said; "can he not read—no books?
> Quoit, tennis, ball—no games? Nor deals in that
> Which men delight in, martial exercise?"
>
> TENNYSON: *The Princess.*

No. 3 of the detailed instructions drawn up by the far-seeing Major Frere for Alured's guidance on joining was to this effect:—

"3. Call upon the adjutant, and beg of him to provide you with a good servant. A respectable old soldier if possible."

Draycott being evilly disposed towards Alured at first, had told him to fish for himself; he did not keep a registry office, the adjutant said. Whereupon Davidson found a man for Alured, Grimes by name, No. 2847, Theophilus Grimes; a soldier of fifteen years' service, with a fine weather-beaten face, somewhat discoloured by time and the tropics. He was more or less broken down by the continuous strain of these heavy fifteen years. "Sentry-go" once a week, and drink once an hour, must have its effect upon the constitution in the end. Not that Grimes was a drunkard. Far from it. He had three good-conduct badges, each of which he had earned nobly by the strength of his head. When the other men fell into the clutches of the sergeant of the guard, Grimes carried his liquor bravely to his barrack-room, and was half asleep before tattoo roll-call began.

On the departure of the 145th for the East, Grimes had been declared unfit for active service. He had remained, therefore, at the depot, helping, as old soldiers do, to train recruits by their advice and example. Grimes looked upon his master as a recruit, whom he was bound to dry-nurse and instruct.

It was Grimes himself who brought in Alured's hot water the morning after the ball at Moynehan. His fairy footfall soon awakened his master, for Grimes, seeking to do honour to himself and his profession, had taken into wear that morning his last issued ammunition boots. They were of a stiff uncompromising material, and might have been made by the armourer-sergeant; creaking at each move till the very windows rattled and vibrated at the noise, their aggrieved owner apostrophizing them at intervals thus :—

"Is it grease ye want? Bad luck to you—and you won't take the blacking yet." "*Quiet*, will you?" "Make less noise or I'll have you off." And sometimes with a long-drawn sigh he murmured, "Oh! me boots. This is no place, sure, for store boots."

But all the time Grimes was taking stock of the room and its contents. Naturally the mansions of the great were not among his daily experiences. I doubt very much whether he had seen the inside of a large country house before. But it was a confirmed habit with this astute old soldier to depreciate everything he came across. He had examined his master's kit the very first day, with severely critical eyes. Declared that them boots would never do at all. They were too narrow. And the uniform clothes were all too loose. And the blacking brushes (provided by Messrs. Jobson), were just rubbish compared with those in the quartermaster's store. "You'll have to give that sword away, sir. It won't do for the Crimayer." "Lord save us! and is this the new pattern shakoo-hat-cap? You can't go to parade in this rigga-my-dandy. It's the first that's come to these barracks, and the men'll all be laughing in the ranks, sir." And when the boxes had been inspected and their contents condemned, other things got their turn. Ballybanagher and its products, natural and artificial were roundly abused. The milk called pig's wash; the bread, bran; the people, savages. Alured was told that the adjutant was "no drill." "Nor yet Sergeant Gaskitt. There's none of them fit to carry the pace-stick for Lance-Corporal Raper;" who was drill instructor to the squad in which, years ago, Grimes had learnt his exercises. The messman was a villain, and Mrs. Moriarty, who was to do Alured's washing, "an old soldier." She'd rob him of the very shirts off his back; and wash the sheets into holes, and "divil a darn in the socks."

As soon as Grimes recovered his first astonishment at Moynehan, he attacked the bedroom furniture.

"A tin foot-pan for a bath. It ought to be mahogany. And not a bootjack, nor a hearth-brush, nor yet glove-trees; and the delf!—"

"Shut up, you old ass!" cried Alured from his bed.

"Are you awake, sir? I thought you were sleeping."

"Who could sleep with you dancing the fandango about the room like an elephant with the erysipelas? What time is it? When did you come over? Is it all right about my leave?"

"There's no rouse sounding in this house. It was near eight when I got here, and it was like a sementerry."

"That'll do, that'll do. Have you filled my bath?"

"I could get no water. And there's nothing but a foot-pan, which wouldn't hold your right leg—let alone your whole body, *sotto voce*, small as ye are."

"Why, you great idiot, don't you see that marble bath in the end of the room?"

"That a bath? Sure I took it for the sink. And it's two men's work to fill that tank. I must ask for a fatigue party."

"Turn on the tap, and it'll fill I daresay. But look sharp; I want to get up."

"There's a letter for you from the dee-pot."

It was a line from Draycott to say he could stay till Monday, and that Grimes had got a pass for the same period.

"Have you brought all I want?"

"Every stitch, sir. Mess clothes and full dress,—not the shakoo hat, leastways; for as it's the new pattern—"

"No mufti?"

"Not a rag. Would you be wearing the like in a duke's castle?"

"By George! of all the owls—do you think I ought to turn out as if for a full-dress parade? How did you get here?"

"On a car, sir."

"Then get the car, and go back to barracks as fast as you can. Bring me all my plain clothes."

"Which, sir?"

"All;" and Alured turned over for a second sleep.

Moynehan Castle was one of the pleasantest houses in the three kingdoms. There was always a party in the house; a crowd of girls, and a dozen men. Everybody did as he liked. Fun and amusement were the order of the day. Now a concert; next night they improvised tableaux; on the following day a whole troop turned out to hunt with the Moynehan hounds. Then came a frost, and they skated or played golf on the ice, or prepared a theatrical performance, or begged Lady Moynehan to light up the ballroom and give them a dance. This very ball to which Alured had been invited had been started suddenly, just to give the young ladies a fillip. In everything Lady Moynehan herself took the lead. She was the life and soul of the place. His lordship was a dear old man; small, chirpy, with bright apple cheeks, and snow white whiskers, cut very precisely; not very active now, although for years he had hunted his own hounds. At times quite *hors de combat* with the gout, at others he hopped about his garden like a bird, or took much interest in his stables. If he had not been such a thoroughly amiable, attractive old gentleman, people might have been disposed to call him a cipher in his own house, for the active duty of doing the honours of Moynehan devolved upon his wife. But she always seemed to defer to him, whenever he made his appearance among the guests.

It was past midday before any of the party appeared at breakfast. Lady Moynehan was one of the first, accompanied by the Tremenheere girls, and one or two other favourites whom she had picked up on the way down stairs.

"Some men want so much sleep," said she.

"The boys are worse," cried Bob Tremenheere. "Your young friend turned in long before any of us, and he's not put in an appearance yet."

"Perhaps he's too shy to come down all alone. I wish, Captain Tremenheere you'd run up and see if he's all right? Do you mind?"

Good-natured Bob started off, and found Alured half dressed, waiting for Grimes' return.

"Breakfast is nearly over."

"I've got no clothes."

"Didn't your servant come?"

"Yes; and brought nothing but uniform."

"What a joke! Shall I lend you some mufti, or will you appear in your red coat?"

"He ought to be back soon. I think I'll wait."

"As you please. I'll go back and tell Lady Moynehan."

When Alured got down, the breakfast-room was almost deserted. But Lady Moynehan came in, and apologised for not having waited.

"Why didn't you put on your uniform, Mr. Frere? It wouldn't have mattered. I've no doubt it suits you."

Alured blushed.

"They'd have thought it so odd, Captain Tremenheere and the men. We never wear uniform, you know, more than we can help."

"It's nothing to be ashamed of, I'm sure. I wish you would, of a night especially. At my balls the men look like undertakers always."

After breakfast, Lady Moynehan said, "The gentlemen have all gone off to shoot or to ride. What would you like to do?"

"Anything."

"Would it bore you to come and help us

ladies? We're going to arrange a charade for to-night. Can you act?"

"I have acted a little—at home."

"And do you know any good words? You'll be quite a treasure."

It was a charming retreat, that ladies' morning-room at Moynehan. Being set apart for Lady Moynehan's private use, no one entered it except by special invitation. Away from the ordinary reception rooms, its windows looked upon a private lawn, guarded by tall trees. On one side, wide doors of plate glass led to a conservatory, crammed always with the choicest plants. Nor was there any lack within the room of brilliant colours. Its decorations were "harlequin." Although the hangings were lemon silk studded with pretty pink roses, and the wood mostly maple and birch, crimson, orange, and purple met the eye here and there in rugs, cushions, Turkey carpet, Moorish footstools, Austrian blankets, and Spanish mule-cloths. The effect, if bizarre, was not unpleasing; and there was relief in the broad white margins of the exquisite water-colours that hid half the walls. Variety as ample was to be seen in the shape of chair and lounge. To suit every taste was the first and only study. Those who preferred fauteuils, soft and downy, with wide hospitable arms, found them. If any prim miss sought to do penance in a *prie-dieu* chair for confession or orisons neglected, she could be accommodated with a seat having a back as stiff and uncompromising as the teaching of her own model divine. There were long roomy sofas for real idlers, who asked only to be undisturbed while others read aloud; and more than one cunningly devised ottoman, just adapted for a very private *tête à-tête* talk.

When Lady Moynehan introduced Alured to this sanctum, he found it half full of young ladies. They were all cutting and contriving, putting their heads together to devise costumes for the evening's charade. Little Millicent was there too, and she welcomed her friend very warmly.

"Did you wonder why I never came back last night?" she asked innocently. "How long did you wait?"

Alured felt that he looked guilty, and knew

that Lady Moynehan's eye was upon him. What was he to say? He had not learnt as yet that perfect command of countenance which is the wages of years of hard service in the wars of society. But he remembered his promise, and it behoved him to give a loyal answer.

"I came out almost directly after you. Did they send you to bed?"

"Yes, aunt did," replied Millicent, pointing crossly to Lady Moynehan.

"Oh, Lady Moynehan!" Alured exclaimed. "What a shame! Why didn't you let her stay up and play with me? You know that was the only reason you asked me to the ball."

This raised a gentle laugh around; and he was rewarded for his promptitude by a grateful approving smile. Then the business in hand was proceeded with. Alured proved indeed a treasure. With some artistic and dramatic taste, as yet hardly developed, he was able to suggest or improve. Then he sketched roughly the design of a dress, which brought several pretty heads to bend over him, and caress him with sweet words of praise.

"Why, you can draw quite nicely," said Lady Moynehan. "Have you ever learnt from any one good? Rivière, or Leitch, or Skinner Prout?"

Alured had not even heard their names.

"I'm very fond of it. But I only had a few lessons—at school."

"I must take you in hand myself. Harding taught me what little I know."

"Draw me a picture for my dress," said little Millicent. "Do, Mr. Frere; please, do."

"I want to teach him to dance," interposed Fanny Tremenheere. "Come away, Mr. Frere, and get it over."

Alured got up very obediently.

"I should have thought, Fanny, you'd had enough of dancing last night."

"That was pleasure; this is duty."

"How many lessons will make me perfect?" asked Alured, when in a more retired room they were prepared to begin, with a good-natured dowager at the piano.

"We'll see."

After the first turn or two, Miss Tremenheere, said "I only brought you in here to get you out of mischief. Those people will spoil you."

"Nonsense."

"Yes, they will. And I thought you promised to learn to shoot and ride and be a man. Bob's quite ready to teach you. Don't stop in here like a milksop with us women. Go out, and behave like a man. We women will like you all the better for it."

"Upon my word, I believe you're right."

"I know I am."

Next time she met Lady Moynehan, this admirable instructress of youth said, "I've been telling our little friend that he'll never get on if he lets himself be coddled amongst us women."

"Why, Fanny, you seem to take an extraordinary interest in Mr. Frere."

"Perhaps I'm not the only person. But he's so nice and fresh and innocent."

"Such a thorough little gentleman," added the other. "I'm sure he's as chivalrous and honourable as he's good-looking."

Perhaps Lady Moynehan was thinking upon her secret, and of Alured as its depositary.

"But you're quite right," she went on; "it won't do to let him be spoiled. I wonder why it is that a woman must spoil everything she really likes? Look at Millicent with her cat: she nearly smothers it half the day with kisses. Snap the Skye is always carried about in somebody's arms. I ruin my mare's digestion by surfeits of sugar. I believe I should kill dear Lord Moynehan with kindness, only he's too wise to let me doctor him."

"Wives generally spoil their husbands."

"I hope you may have one to spoil too, Fanny, before long. However, it's quite clear we must put Mr. Frere into your brother Bob's hands. But we can't do much to-day, and to-morrow's Sunday."

"And he goes on Monday?"

"Yes; so we'd better make the most of him while we can," said Lady Moynehan, with a laugh.

"But you'll ask him again?"

"If he likes to come."

The long and the short of it was, Alured's education was taken in hand by his new friends, ably assisted by such under-masters as Bob Tremenheere, with the keepers and head groom of Moynehan Castle. The first short visit was followed by another and another. Always thoughtful and kind, Lady Moynehan guessed that the ensign's shallow purse would not stand frequent car-hire. A Moynehan dogcart was despatched therefore to fetch him and take him back. Nothing was complete at the Castle without Alured. He was in and out of the house like a tame cat; never forgetting, however, Miss Tremenheere's advice not to tie himself quite to the ladies' petticoats. He could see himself that a man who shirked manly sports to dally in drawing-rooms might win success, to a certain point, among his charming friends; but he was likely to be more than unpopular among men. He might become a "ladies' man," but he would never be a "man's man." I expect most high-spirited lads think more of the good opinion of men, however luscious the doses of flattery which women may administer. So Alured accepted a mount from Lord Moynehan's stable, and hunted as often as he could get the chance. Boyish pluck and young bones soon gave him a home in the saddle. Although he could not hope to be in the first flight of a hard-riding country, he took all that came in his way, and often saw as much of a run as his betters in the pigskin. He braved the displeasure of the keepers, and blazed away in the covers so much, that at last he got to hold his gun straight.

And it was very pleasant for him to be so much at Moynehan—nicer still to be frequently in Lady Moynehan's society. There was joy in his heart always when he got one of her kind notes of invitation; it was better still when she herself, with Millicent at her side, came to the barracks for him in the carriage. How they sketched and painted indoors, and practised and played all kinds of music!

These were bright days indeed for the boy; halcyon days, with smooth water and a fair wind to carry the young craft far out and onward on his long voyage.

CHAPTER XI.

THE ROUTE.

"Yo, señor, soy medico, y estoy asalariado en esta insula para serlo de los gobernadores della, y miro por su salud mucho mas que por la mia, estudiando de noche y de dia."
Don Quijote.

"I am the doctor, paid to be such, to the governors of this island, and, studying night and day, look to their health more than my own."

"Hurrah, boys! The route's come."

"For whom?"

"A draft of officers of the 145th, to join head-quarters. Old Draycott showed me the letter."

"How many are to go?"

"Half a dozen subalterns."

"Four lieutenants and two ensigns," Draycott added, coming in just then. "To proceed to Gravesend forthwith for embarkation. Reporting themselves, etc., etc."

"It'll take you in, Frere," said Bulger, who was also to be one of the party.

"Who's going to the Crimea?" asked

Starkie, in his deep voice, from the far end of the room. "Frere?"

"Yes; he's in the lot."

"Ah, indeed;" remarked the surgeon, drily. Then to a mess-waiter, in a brusque, fierce tone, "Confound you, take this filth away. Take it down-stairs. Ask him if he has the effrontery to call that a grill. I'd make better with bread and milk and oatmeal. So you're going to the wars, young Frere, eh? aha! to the wars aha! They'll have you on your back before you've been there a week, and they'll cut your liver out—and eat it probably afterwards, devilled. I hope it'll eat better than what this beast of a mess-man calls a grill. You've had the measles, I suppose?"

"I don't know, really."

"And whooping cough, and croup, and all that? Yes? I daresay you have. But have you had dysentery and typhus, and gun-shot wounds, and sword-cuts, and syncope, and tetanus, and cholera?" His voice rose to a roar as he enumerated each calamity. "Do you know what it is to lie on the damp ground all night in soaking rain, or to march with a pile of bread and beef on your back, beside your accoutrements, till your throat is dry and rough, like a new sponge, and your head is fit to burst under the blazing heat? Do you know what it is to be in a raging fever, with no food to suit your pampered appetite but pickled sardines or fried salt pork —and hard tough biscuit, instead of tapioca and arrowroot and pap? Not you. Bah! You'd better go home again. It's murder, neither more nor less; and I should be an accessory before the fact if I let you go out."

Just at this time the side bones of a turkey reappeared, as hot as cayenne could make them, and as the grill seemed to stimulate his palate a little, Starkie gave up talking, and addressed himself vigorously to his food. Frere flushed indignantly at what the doctor said, but did not expostulate. It would have been useless; everybody laughed at Starkie's jokes.

But it was no joke when later that day an orderly came to fetch Mr. Frere to the colonel's office. There, in state, sat the personage in chief command; an austere man, who scowled at the youngsters as if they were his personal enemies, but who was as tender-hearted and affectionate, really, as any woman. Alured had entered that office once only before. It had fallen to his lot to "take a defaulter" before the colonel; that is, to stand by with the character-book, and assist in the disposal of prisoners. Some one had told him it was the correct thing to draw his sword and march in like an executioner in front of his defaulter. This he had done most religiously, to the great delight of the lookers-on; but the scolding he had got on that occasion, was still fresh in his mind at this his second visit, and he waited trembling to hear what was in store for him now.

"Your name, Mr. Frere, has been 'returned' to me, to go with the draft. I have sent for you to tell you that I cannot permit you to proceed to the Crimea."

"Oh, sir, why not?" asked Alured piteously, his eyes filling with tears.

"The doctor says—"

Alured looked up at once, and for the first time became aware that Starkie was there standing beside the colonel. He, then, was the enemy who had done this thing.

The surgeon now spoke.

"Mr. Frere, in my opinion, colonel, is unfit for active service. He is much too young, his constitution is still unformed, and he has not the physique to withstand privations."

"Physique? Why, sir," cried Alured, wiping his eyes, "I never was ill in my life. It's true I'm only just sixteen; but I'll run any man in the battalion round the barrack square or walk the doctor to Knockalofty and back. Don't, please, sir, don't, mind what he says; he doesn't know anything about it,—not half as much as I do myself."

The colonel smiled at Mr. Frere's arguments, and looked inquiringly at the doctor. Old Starkie merely shrugged his shoulders.

"I think we'd better let him go," said the chief.

"As you please, sir. He won't live there a week I expect."

"That's my affair;" put in Alured.

"It certainly is your own look-out," remarked the colonel.

"You see if I don't live," added Alured, almost snapping his fingers in Starkie's face.

"Very well, Mr. Frere," said Colonel Willoughby, at last. "You shall go. It would would be a pity to baulk you; and I like your spirit. Captain Draycott, his name may be included in the list for the quarter-master general." And with these words the interview broke up.

Outside of the office, Alured flew at old Starkie.

"Why did you try to put a spoke in my wheel? I'm sure I never did you any harm."

"Harm boy? No, no harm. But I like you too much to wish you under the sod."

It was not often that the man threw anybody a civil word. Alured felt that, after all, the doctor's interference was kindly meant. And he was to go—that was enough! He was fairly beside himself with delight.

"Are you going to say good-bye to your swell friends, over at that castle, or cockloft, or whatever it is?" asked Starkie.

"I want to, but I have so little time."

"I will drive you over if you like, and pick

you up on my way back. My trap's at the door. Run along and dress."

Alured had no idea that this curious creature, whose society he had somewhat shunned, could make himself so agreeable. All along the road he poured forth story after story, and joke upon joke—most of them directed against the softer sex.

"They'll be wanting you to marry one of them one of these days. Some duchess's daughter, Lady Barbara Balderdash, or a dowager marchioness."

"No such luck. These people look higher than a marching ensign."

"I don't believe it. The higher the rank, the more they don't care. I know it. I'll swear to it. I've seen it," roared Sparkie.

"Not often."

"Well, not often; but once, in my own experience. Why, man alive, I had a groom once,—and a precious scoundrel he was,—it was when I was doing duty with the Guards, and this fellow, this flunky was married to a lady. Ran off with her, by George, from her father's house; and her father, lord something or other, with a lot of daughters all first chop."

" Did you call on your groom's wife, Starkie, and ask her tea, to meet her own relations ? "

" No. But I bundled the man neck and crop out of the stable when I found him selling my oats. Not that it was easy to shake him off. He came whining back to say his wife was dying, and that she hadn't the commonest necessaries of life. So I went and saw them, and gave her the benefit of my professional advice such as it is."

" Did she die ? "

" Meaning that for me, eh ? As much as to say I killed her ? No; I pulled her through, young chap. There was a baby besides, which lived all right too."

" Did you ever see anything of the people again ? "

" Well, not exactly. But, when I came from India in '51, I used to think I saw the groom's wife sometimes; in a carriage generally—but I never bothered my head about her. It was evident she didn't want any help, or she'd have asked for it. That's the way with women. They sponge upon you, if it suits them, turn you inside out like an orange; and when sucked dry, they chuck you away.

"But here we are at the lodge gates. Shall I take you up to the door or drop you here?"

"Won't you come in and make their acquaintance?"

"What I? You must be rather out in your calculations about me. Not a step, boy. I hate women, the whole kit of them, from countesses to kitchen-maids. But I may as well drive in."

Alured jumped down at the door, and met Lady Moynehan coming out from the hall, accompanied by the dogs.

"Why, Mr. Frere," she said, holding out her hand with good-natured warmth, "it's an age since you were near us. You're quite a stranger. Will you come in? I was only going out with my private pack into the shrubbery. Which do you perfer?"

At the same moment Starkie's voice was heard from the trap,—"I'll call for you in an hour's time, Frere, if that will suit."

"Yes; very well."

And then the doctor drove off.

Now I have already said there was something peculiar about Starkie's voice. It was a deep-toned, massive voice, that made an echo like a clanging ponderous bell.

No sooner had Lady Moynehan heard it, than she grew strangely agitated. Her lips blanched and her hands seemed to quiver with excitement.

"Ah!" she exclaimed with a long-drawn sigh, as soon as Starkie was out of sight, "I felt just as if some one had been treading on my grave. Do you know the feeling, Mr. Frere? Goose flesh, and an involuntary shudder. Come, Let us walk it off."

Lady Moynehan stepped on briskly. No one knew better than she that sharp exercise meant health, and that health meant a satin skin and clear complexion. Every day, wet or dry, accompanied by a troop of dogs, she made the circuit of the park.

Alured told her he had come to say good-bye.

"Oh, dear me! are you going away so soon? I do hope you won't get killed or come to any harm. It seems such a shame to send you to the Crimea. You are so much too young."

Alured and the countess had become very

fast friends since that first curious passage of arms at the ball, and he, boy-like, had fallen desperately in love—quite innocently be it understood—with this magnificent woman who was so much older than he was. Not that he allowed it to himself, or thought of her otherwise than as a queen; she was so grand, so beautiful, of such high rank, so immeasurably his superior. But it hurt him rather that she should speak of him almost as a child. He did not quite know what he wanted, but he longed for some opportunity to show himself a man.

"You are so very young," repeated Lady Moynehan.

"They said the same, Lady Moynehan, at the barracks. But I beat them, doctor and all. That was the doctor who drove me over here."

"That man?" said her ladyship, laying her hand nervously on Alured's arm. "What's his name?"

"Starkie."

"Starkie, Starkie," as if musing. "What an odd name; and what a strange-looking man. Do you like him very much?"

"I believe he's a good fellow at bottom, but he's curious in his ways—lives hard and—"

Alured was going to say that the doctor sometimes drank more than was good for him, but it seemed like telling tales out of school.

His hesitation had been lost on his companion. Evidently heedless of his words, Lady Moynehan walked on. The dogs fawned upon her, and jumped upon her dress without rebuke.

"Let us go back to the house," she said abruptly. "You would like to see Lord Moynehan perhaps."

"And Miss Millicent?"

"Oh Millicent, of course. You shall make your adieus in the tenderest language if you like. We'll all look the other way. But I really am very sorry you are going; we seem to have got to be such good friends. And you won't forget us?"

"Not easily, Lady Moynehan, or all your kindness."

"You must come back, Mr. Frere; come back a general, if possible."

"A live donkey is better than a dead general, they say."

"If you like to call yourself names, well and good. But you are the last person I should call a donkey. Far from it; and you ought to do very well in the world." She led the way into her own cosy room, and sank into her favourite seat, a low chair by the fire, as soon as she had touched the bell. "Tell Miss Millicent," she said to the groom of the chambers, "that Mr. Frere is here; and is his lordship in his room?"

"He is, my lady."

"Ask him if he will come and have some tea. I always take tea about this time of the day, Mr. Frere; will you have some too? Yes? Tea," to the servant, who disappeared.

It was a pleasant little party. First the bright-eyed maid rushed in; then the old lord, with slow and painful step, came to bid the young man God speed, and was full of courtly interest in his future.

"I dare say I can give you some introduction out there. De Courcey is an old friend of mine, and Cawthorpe, and Thorold. They were in the Guards with me years ago."

"A gentleman is waiting. He has called for Mr. Frere," said the footman, coming in.

"My time is up, Lady Moynehan."

"Your friend would not care to come in, would he?" she asked.

"He is an old bear, and hates ladies' society."

"Then he had better stay outside," said her ladyship gaily. "And must you really go?"

Good-byes are always sad to say; and these kind people reminded Alured somewhat of the dear ones at home. His orders to start for the Crimea had come so suddenly that it had been impossible for him to go to Scaggleton. Obliged thus to leave England without seeing his mother and sisters again, the ladies of Moynehan, for the moment, took their place. But gulping down his sorrow, he exclaimed,—

"Starkie will be getting savage. I am keeping him in the cold all this time."

"Good-bye, then; good-bye. Take care of yourself, Mr. Frere."

"And come back, Mr. Frere; mind you come back."

"I hope you'll prosper," said Lord Moynehan, giving him his hand. "I'll send the letter over to the barracks to-night. *Bonvoyage.*"

The ladies came out into the hall to see the last of him. Then he swung himself up to Starkie's side, and they drove off.

"Who was that we met at the hall door?" asked the doctor, as soon as they were once more on the high road.

"Lady Moynehan."

"*Lady* Moynehan. Not to put too fine a point upon it, the Earl of Moynehan's wife?"

"Do you know her? Have you ever seen her before?"

"Perhaps I have, and perhaps I haven't. It's no affair of yours, youngster. She may be like some one I knew long ago. Will that satisfy you?"

Frere for answer launched forth into a panegyric of the countess, which lasted them all the way back to barracks.

It did not occur to him, simple youth, to put two and two together. Had he been as clever as you, reader, he might have constructed a pretty mystery from the fragments put into his hands at Moynehan Castle.

CHAPTER XII.

THE VOYAGE OUT.

"And oh the bitter tears we wept
    In those our days of fame;
The dread that o'er our heartstrings crept
    With every post that came.
The home affections waged and lost
    In every far-off fray!
The price that British glory cost—
    Ah! take the sword away."
                      PRAED.

ALURED FRERE and his companions on reaching Gravesend, found the *Sailor Queen,* their transport, out in the stream, but by no means ready for sea. Freight littered the deck, mingled with coal dust, live stock, and baggage. Altogether the *Sailor Queen* seemed quite unfit to rule waves more boisterous than a ripple on the Thames.

There was no one to receive them; every one was too busy, and they had scaled the ship's side unnoticed. After some difficulty and delay the "chief officer" was dug out from a cabin which bore his name, on the upper deck. The chief was anxious to be civil, but "unfort'ntly rather mops and brooms," as he said himself. They gathered from his indistinct speech that the ship could not sail till next day.

"'Old on, gen'lm'n, 'l ask the p-purser," he hiccoughed, as he leant with drunken tenacity over the main hatch, and roared down "'Ere 'Arry, 'Arry! drop them ullages and rot-rot down in the 'old. Come up and tell the gen'l'mn—off'shers, and gen'l'mn—when ship's shready for sh-ea."

"'Arry," the purser, was also supercargo. For the voyage of the *Sailor Queen* to the East was a trading venture, and she carried passengers only as a secondary business.

As "Mi's'r Jeel," the chief officer introduced the purser; but his real name was Geil, and he was better known as Jellybags. A little, round, podgy man, young still, but over fat for his age. It was his first voyage as supercargo, and as he was part owner, some importance attached itself to him—at least in his own eyes.

" Hi am surprised, Mr. Helmouth, you should have disturbed me in the midst of a 'tally.'"

"'Ang the tally, 'Arry; speak to the gen'l'm." Then, in reply to Alured, Mr. Geil condescended to say,—"We shall in most probability descend the river by to-morrow's tyide. The hevening ty-ide."

"Is it necessary for us to remain on board?" asked Gregson.

"Ham I to understand that you hair provided with passages in this steam SHIP?"

"You hair," replied Alured, mimicking his voice. "Pray, say whether we are to expect an answer to-night?"

"I de-clyine, gentlemen, to be more communicative, and refer you to the captain; he's at present from home."

"Oh, come lads," cried Dalrymple; "let's go back to the village; we shall get no good out of this little cad."

"Cad, sir!" exclaimed Jellybags, advancing threateningly at Alured, whom he thought the easiest to lick, being the youngest of the party. "Was that hoffensive, brutally hoffensive hepithet haddressed to me?"

"I'll pitch you over the side if you come an inch nearer," said Alured.

"Drop it, 'Arry, drop it. Of course he knows, an' I know, an' everybody knows, that you're only old Jellybags."

"I shall demand han hapology—categorically hapologetic, when you return gentlemen. Your language has been most huntemperate."

Alured and the others turned on their heels and left him. Hurrying back to shore they took the first train back to London, determined to take a last taste of the pleasures of civilized life.

It was the strangest night's fun, and the most miserable apology for a debauch that ever truant schoolboys indulged in. Yet Alured, mindful of his meeting with Pierpoint, fancied that for that night only he too was a "man about town." Heaven save the mark! Had these youngsters been brought before a select committee of Arthur's, Boodle's, Brook's, or Pratt's, they would hardly have passed muster. Gregson, on the strength of his approaching apotheosis as a Crimean hero, had thought it right to let his beard grow, but it was still in the stubbly recent stage, and his chin was black and unlovely to look upon. Routh, too, had been determined to cast himself adrift from the conventionalities of life as soon as practicable, and he had made a football of his hat and hat-box as he entered Athenmore station, adorning himself with a regimental forage-cap instead. But the others had refused to travel with him in this "cocktail" apparel, so he disguised the badge and cap with an oil silk cover, till he looked like a railway guard. Little Bulger, the third of the party, had missed his baggage, "sent it to the wrong 'otel," he said; and this was his excuse for wearing a dirty shirt, but he might have bought a clean collar, if it had only been a paper one, nor would it have cost him much to wash his face, or to cover his vulgar hands with a pair of cheap gloves. But Bulger was the leading man of the party, on the strength of his knowledge of life. It was he who marched them to an hotel in Covent Garden, where they were refused admittance promptly. Without baggage, and with Bulger as a spokesman, they did not inspire confidence among hotel-keepers. At last Bulger said he knew of a snug little crib somewhere off Soho, and thither they repaired in a body. Here they were more successful. But the money for their night's lodging had to be paid down in advance. Fortunately they were all in funds. The morning they left Ballybanagher the paymaster had handed to each a small pile of golden sovereigns—six months' field allowance paid in advance, and it was this windfall they were now eager to spend.

It would be as well, perhaps, to draw a veil over their adventures. Suffice it to say that they dined at a swell eating-house—in Soho; went to a swell theatre also—in Soho, and to swell concert-rooms, and swell billiard-rooms, and swell supper-rooms, and, as Bulger explained to a friend next day on board the *Sailor Queen*, kept it up till all was blue.

Oh, the curse of a vicious associate! the curse of gas-lit, flaring, midnight London, to poison and blight the innocence of unsuspecting youth! Poor Alured was none the better for tasting the pleasures of town. It was not till next afternoon that he could pull himself together, and swallow breakfast. Then they journeyed again to Gravesend, and once more trod the deck of the *Sailor Queen*. Such as she was—a coasting-boat, meant at times to cross the Channel in favourable weather,—this great steamship was ready for sea. Had she been told that she was now to face the Black Sea, the Bay of Biscay, and Mediterranean gales, she would have shrieked out a vigorous veto from all her creaking timbers. But the anchor was a-trip, steam up, the pilot aboard; the captain came off in a shore boat with one of the owners; passenger after passenger clambered up to the deck; and all was ready.

Frere, Bulger, Routh, Gregson, and Dalrymple, were standing together, and the 145th mustered all present. No, not all present. Where was Skinner? Skinner, an old lieutenant, who had lived much to himself at Ballybanagher, and when the route had come, had travelled to Gravesend alone.

Now, discerning his absence, one man asserted that he had bolted, gone off, deserted. Another swore he would be tried by court martial, as sure as the trees grew little apples.

"You'll give him a moment's law; won't you, captain?" asked Alured, soft-hearted.

" Give whom ?"

" Skinner of ours."

"Hain't he made out the number of his mess? Then, by thunder, he'll lose his passage. I couldn't wait now for the commander-in-chief, or the queen of Sheba, or my own father."

He mentioned the three in a breath, as if they were all nearly connected.

" But if he loses his passage—"

"*Sailor Queen*, ahoy!" came from a boat alongside—a boat bearing three passengers, Skinner among them.

"You'll miss your passage," cried Frere. But Skinner paid no heed to the lad's words. All his attention was engrossed by a person who sat by his side in a paroxysm of grief. It was his bride. Just one short week of married bliss, then Eastward, ho! This Skinner had been engaged for years, and was waiting till he was a captain to marry. But a slender provision even that for matrimony. Yet had he left the depot when the sudden route had come, to marry out of hand. Poor souls! What did they reck of the lookers-on that crowded the deck of the *Sailor Queen*? What to them, in that moment of intense agony had been even a million eyes bent upon them with curious intrusive gaze? For her there was no one else in all the world but Archibald, and he was going from her, perhaps never to return. To her the interest of life seemed almost at an end. For him there was little to hope for. The circle of a grey uneventful career had been completed; apart from her there could be neither happiness nor comfort, no sensation but one long yearning desire to be reunited to the woman he loved. Of what avail to protract the bitter moment? The words must be spoken; Captain Costabadie would wait no longer.

"God bless you, my own darling!"

"Oh, Archibald! oh, my love! how can I part with you! Say you will come back—only say you will come back."

"If God wills," said Skinner, taking off his hat solemnly.

There were many youths and hardened men too standing there, unwilling witnesses to the scene, who echoed the poor fellow's words, and added a silent amen to his prayer.

They were soon speeding along the river,

and until the channel widened, took part in the grand regatta for ever in progress on the Thames. Presently the sun went down—setting upon Old England, and Skinner's sorrow, and his wife's lonely anguish, upon the hushed quiet of many an English home owning a son embarked that night in the *Sailor Queen*. The bright luminary disappeared, not with cold heartless tones, but in a blaze of splendour, warming up with hope and courage the hearts of men, tingeing with the reflection of his royal presence the vassal clouds that waited obsequious on his exit, and flushing with rosy pride the dancing waves that last had felt his smile. Lights on either bank began to flash and sparkle, at first with timid radiance, as if it had been intolerable conceit to seek to vie with the bright effulgence yet scarcely passed away, then with more assurance as the darkness came on apace. The world was narrowed now for those on board the *Sailor Queen* to the ship itself. The ceaseless play of the engines, the red light that rose above the funnel, the movement of sailors and passengers, the casting of the log, or the striking of the hours,—beyond these, all things were shut out by the black night.

A very notable voyage this for Alured. The mere transition from his native land to scenes entirely different in character and local colour, must alone have given him food for thought. Each day there was something new. After a prosperous run down Channel, they left late one evening the Start Point under their lee— the last English land. Then came the Bay of Biscay, like a terrible dream, from which Alured woke to hear that the ship had been in danger more than once. But with Cape St. Vincent and the Spanish coast, brighter days dawned; skies a deeper blue, seas a brighter purple, washing the base of mountains, whose summits neared the clouds. Here was smooth water; an infinite boon after the tossings of the "Bay." At length, passing Cape Trafalgar so close that they might have thrown a biscuit on shore, they entered one splendid spring morning the far-famed Straits of Hercules. Europe and Africa, on either side, seemed to be stretching out their hands as if in salutation; each continent on tip-toe with a thousand miles of country, waste or populated, behind to keep them from toppling over. Sea and heaven smiled upon the meeting. The first lay with a smooth face beneath the bright burning gaze of the sun, placidly dozing on in sleek happiness unruffled by a breeze, unrippled by a current, stirred only by the dipping wings of the sea-birds or the gambols of a porpoise. On one side tall blue mountains melting away into the far distance; on the other, mountains bluer, taller, and more remote, while the Great Rock, Tarik's Rock,—Gibraltar,—a focus, as it were, of all this beauty, lay in the centre, interposing like a stone door right across the gateway of the Mediterranean.

Captain Costabadie had apparently no wish to consult but his own wayward fancy as to his course. From Gibraltar he steered for Algiers, not because it was on his road, but because some one had asked what the place was like, and he did not want to be compelled to confess twice that he had never seen it. The chief officer arrogated to himself the same powers. He bore up one night for Cagliari in the island of Sardinia, because the liquor was running short, and he had a fancy that light Italian wines might suit his palate. At Malta they halted of course. Jellybags had plenty of business to transact in the Strada Stretta. But these days at Malta were full of excruciating torture to Alured, for he had there met a young officer like himself, who had been actually detained at Malta, as too young to go on. Frere ran back from Joe Micalef's straight to the *Sailor Queen*, and hid himself. He neglected altogether the introductions given him by his father and Lord Moynehan. He did not dare go on shore to present them. And one was to the general in command, Alured's chief enemy! It was not till they were once more at sea that he breathed freely.

There was some talk of making for Alexandria, but a naval officer among the passengers who was anxious to join his ship before Sebastopol, began to talk about "charter parties," and "demurrage" for delays. Jellybags grew frightened. The further he got from England the more he respected the powers of war, and those who followed its trade. But he made a stand at Syra, in the Grecian archipelago, though there was little trade to be done there except in windmills; and at Constantinople they wasted a week.

At last, one morning, Alured woke in Balaclava harbour.

CHAPTER XIII.

AT THE FRONT.

> " The trumpets sound
> The colours flying are, my boys;
> To fight, kill, or wound,
> May we still be found,
> Content with our hard fare, my boys,
> On the cold ground."

THE *Sailor Queen* lay amidst a forest of masts, in a busy bay, landlocked and sheltered by high hills. Bustle surrounded her. Boats hurrying to and fro, laden with freight, living and dead, merchandize, fruits, sick and wounded, shot and shell.

" There goes Blatherwyck," cries some one, as a man in an old sheepskin coat, and looking like a ghost, is rowed past. " I said he wouldn't last a week out here."

" Going to Scutari."

" Dying of funk probably."

Blatherwyck was one of the Ballybanagher bad bargains. He had shirked so long, that at last they had ordered him to sell or sail. He sailed, and stayed in the Crimea just one week, during which time he obtained a majority without purchase in his regiment.

But by this time the *Sailor Queen* had been boarded by many visitors. It was refreshing to see the air with which the captain and Mister Jellybags did the honours of the ship. These visitors were customers,—officers from "the front," in search of food, clothing, drink,— anything, from paper to pickles. Jellybags was more at home now than he had been at sea. His real trade was barter; his training had been behind a counter, in the mysteries of profit and loss.

"Hexcuse me, major, it's cheap at forty-two the dozen;" and "I couldn't let you have it a halfpenny cheaper;" "They stands us in more than that; they does indeed," were phrases constantly in his mouth. Captain Costabadie presided at the festive board, where sardines and bottled beer were laid out to foster enterprise among the buyers.

Of course there was plenty of news about.

"A sortie last night; the —th bolted."

"Oh come!"

"They *did*. Blessington told me so. I'd have fired into them, by George."

"Like Paddy Geoghan of ours."

"Did he?"

"Yes, faith. We were in support at the Woronzoff road, and a fellow of the Blazers hooked it back from the *chevaux de frise*. Crying for his mother he was. The Russians were in force at the picquet house."

"Well?"

"As he came towards us, Geoghan put up his rifle, and shot him dead."

"What did they do to Geoghan?"

"What 'd you want 'em to do to him? He's shouldering his gun still. They call him 'Paddy Geoghan that shot the Blazer,' that's all."

"Carruthers, of the —th was shot, at the Ovens last night."

"Infernal place. Hot as—"

"An oven."

"Poor joke. But it *is* hot. There's a casualty or two there most nights."

"A casualty" is a military euphemism for a man killed.

"They say there's to be another attack to-morrow."

"Pooh! there's always going to be an attack. I'll believe it when I see it in orders."

"They won't put it in orders; there are too many spies about."

"Spies!" derisively.

"There *are!*" emphatically.

Now although this conversation was swallowed with delight by our friends of the *Sailor Queen*, still Frere and the others of the 145th were anxious to know how they were to get to "the front." Bulger, more forward than the rest, asked at length.

"You can ride up. I'll sell you a pony," answered some one at once.

"So will I," added another and another.

"Can't we take the train?" inquired Bulger.

"What train? the Military Train?"

"No; I mean the railway."

"That's a good idea! Why it only goes to Kadikoi; and there are no officers' tickets on this line."

"And no carriages."

"And no guard's van."

"And no refreshment rooms—I wish there were."

By this time a laugh had been got up at Bulger's expense. They would have got no information had not Frere interposed. Somehow the apple-faced lad, with his bright cheery looks, won friends at once.

"You are going to join the 145th? They are in the Fourth Division. You had better walk. It's only half a dozen miles."

"And our baggage?"

"Leave it at the regimental store in Balaclava. They'll send some mokes down for it from your head-quarters."

No better advice than this, so they landed at once. Did any emotions swell the hearts of these young soldiers as they trod for the first time Crimean soil? Were they conscious that they too, in a humble way, were about to make history; that as simple units they might perhaps add something to the array of facts to be handed down as the deeds of the Crimeans? Not exactly I take it. One youngster was growling at the sun; another at the dust; a third began to wonder where the store was, and if there was any liquor to be got there. But it was impossible even for the most matter-of-fact among them, and this was certainly not our hero, to gaze for the first time on Balaclava without surprise. It was like a great world fair—as if a concourse of nations had come together on pressing business of their own, and bivouacking, or building huts, as suited them best, had stayed to carry it out; a motley crowd, in diverse and many coloured raiment. Soldiers were but sparingly seen, for their work was elsewhere; but among the waggons of the land transport were fatigue parties in dust-coloured tunics, and besides them a sprinkling of horse artillerymen or cavalry troopers, from their camp close at hand, some Sardinians and stray Frenchmen, and no end of Turks. Here and there an occasional T. G.—travelling gentleman—the *nom de guerre* of all amateurs, from the Duke of This or Lord John That, to lowly canteen keepers coining money, or gents travelling for Messrs. Jobson & Co. Hurry was the order of the day—a normal condition for staff officers dashing in and out, for British tars riding borrowed ponies; abnormal and constantly slackening on the part of those lazy races who were compensating Great Britain for voluntary enlistment and the thinned ranks it entails, by doing as little of the dirty work as could be got out of them. All this in the midst of a Babel of languages—Smaitch, Turkish, Greek, Armenian, Dutch, while high above all the din rose strong and superior the Englishman's undisguised and idiomatic invective.

There was a good road by this time to the front, and our friends had no difficulty in piloting themselves along. Every mile brought them to something new, which counteracted the monotony of their march. Now it was Kadikoi, a shanty-town, full of activity, now a camp, or a battery, or another camp. Soon a dull, distant, heavy "thud" began to fall frequently upon the ear; and as they gained at length the summit of the Fedukhine heights, and saw beneath them the camps of the opposing armies, the lines of trench, and beyond again, spread out like a scroll, Sebastopol itself, they understood what was meant by the puff of white smoke, for all the world like a morsel of cotton-wool, and the far-off report that followed it. At last the curtain was up, and they were looking at the performance. Indeed, the last act was already begun. The allies, like hounds, would soon break from scent to view, and Alured was destined to be in at the death.

At the camp of the 145th, every one turned out to greet the new arrivals. Those of the soldiers not too jaded or worn to care for new sensations, came to stare at the reinforcement of young blood and fresh sinew from the old country at home.

"It's good for sore eyes to see an ensign," said old McGuiness, a captain of thirty years' service—one of the very oldest school. "Faix, ye're the only ensigns in the Crimayer."

"They'll not have to wait long for the next step."

"Be japers, they won't. We're bound to the ditches, some of us, to-night, and the Rooshies maybe'll be making cold meat of one or another of us. It's more than a month since we had a casualty in the ridgement."

"Where are you detailed for, McGuiness?"

"I don't know. Greenhill, covering party, advanced trenches, Woronzoff Road, or the cimitery, or some other divilish hot place."

"What's the good of their sending out little chaps like you?" said a voice behind Alured. "You'll be on your back before a week's out, and we'll have to do your duty for you."

Frere looked round to see who it was that gave him such a cordial welcome. The veteran who spoke in such disparaging language of the newly-arrived ensign was not such a very big chap himself: a boy-captain, with a smooth face, smoother than was agreeable to himself, to judge from the care bestowed upon the three hairs that did duty for a beard. But there was a look of kindly interest in his eyes that took all the venom out of his jesting speech.

"Let me introduce you two boys," said old McGuiness. "There's hardly a pin to choose between you. If he's too young to be an ensign, I'll swear you're too young to be a captain."

"You'd have liked promotion as quick as mine, if you could have got it."

"Children like you commanding companies under fire! It's ridiculous. And this young Frere as bad. He won't be able to carry the colour."

" Frere ?"

"Yes; poor Bob's brother."

"You don't mean that? But I ought to have seen the likeness. Your brother and I," said this young man, abruptly, "were always very thick. I dare say he used to mention my name—Kenneth Kensington."

It was not a name likely to be forgotten soon by the Freres.

"Then it was you who brought back the body under fire, and—"

"Don't talk about it. I only did what any one else would have done."

There was a slight pause.

"Have you had any dinner?" Kensington said soon, in an ordinary voice. "Come to my tent. I'm going to dine early. As I'm for the trenches with McGuiness, you can sleep in my bed to-night."

"We were to have had some mutton," he went on, as they sat down to those tough steaks of ration beef, the usual Crimean dinner, "but I couldn't manage it. There's lots of drink, however."

Choice of a dozen liquids rather bewildered Frere; but Kensington decided for him by insisting on champagne.

"They say the Rooshies drink porter with their champagne. Would you like to mix? No? But you must have some grog. I have half-a-dozen rations of rum put by, and lots of lime-juice. I like to take my whack always before I go down to the ditches: it keeps the cold out. By-the-way, you'd better come down and see us by-and-by. It's sure to be a quiet night."

Frere was nothing loth, and, shortly after dark, with Gregson, he started; Joe Candlish, one of the old hands, volunteering to do guide.

From their camp into the valley of the shadow of death was but a step; and along the low ground there was plenty to remind them of the game at which they were playing. All about, choking and crushing down the herbage, lay shot of all sizes, and shapeless fragments of shells. They passed more than one party homeward bound, after twenty-four hours trench duty, glad to turn in at length with whole skins. Every now and then a clatter and a rushing, whistling sound, gave notice of a passing shot; gone as it had come, leaving no track but the rattle it made on the rocks and stones as it bounded onward.

They found McGuiness in reserve at the first parallel, his men lying asleep close up under the gabions. Kensington was detached, down to the Woronzoff Road.

"How are we to get there?" asked Alured.

"You'd better not go, lads. You're not on duty mind. Suppose anything were to happen to you?"

"But I promised Kensington."

"I'll see you through it," said Joe Candlish. "I know the way down."

The three threaded the parallel slowly, stumbling at every yard over men asleep. At the end of the trench was a steep descent, down which they floundered by a sort of covered way, till they reached, at the bottom, the Woronzoff Road.

To their surprise, they found the place in

a fluster. The general commanding the left attack was there, peering over the trench and up the pass. Kensington met his visitors rather coldly, and pointed hurriedly to the general.

The great man at that instant turned and spoke.

"As soon as the enemy advance, Captain Kensington, retire your men slowly from the *chevaux de frise*. There are two guns in position just over us, which will sweep the road. But hold on here, in the second line, to the last. I'll send you more men if you're hard pressed."

He stopped suddenly, for Alured's shooting coat caught his eye.

"Who are these?" asked the general, sharply.

"Friends of mine, who have come down to the trenches for the first time to—"

"Amateurs?"

"No, sir. They are officers of my regiment. They have only just landed."

"You came down here for a lark, I suppose, young gentlemen? I have nothing to do with your larks; and, recollect, you're not on duty. If anything happens to you, it will be your own fault.

"Take my advice," continued the general: "go back to your camp sharp. I don't mind telling you we are expecting a sortie in force, along our whole line. The sentries report heavy columns forming just in front. Back! Go back at once. You must not get into trouble," added the general, speaking kindly to Alured, "by being absent from your colours the first time you're ordered under fire. Your division will be paraded directly, I promise you. In half an hour the whole army will be under arms."

Somewhat abashed, the boys turned and retraced their steps. For all their hurry, they could not regain their camp before the game began. Soon a series of sparks lit up the line of the trenches they had just left, followed by a sharp rattle,—rifle shots barking quick and angrily, like the growls of a house-dog disturbed. Five minutes more, and the 145th had turned out. Officers rapidly inspected pouches, and counted ammunition. The regiment formed up, and was marched to the divisional rallying place; thence the whole mass moved to the engineer park, behind Greenhill. Meanwhile, the turmoil down below continued. The flashing lights lit up half the horizon, and defined clearly the whereabouts of the fight. At times the noise rose or sank, as each side seemed to slacken or renew the struggle. Then all at once it ceased; the enemy had been driven back.

Parade dismissed, Alured would gladly have gone to bed, but the night's excitement was not at an end. He was carried off with the other new arrivals to receive his Crimean baptism. A brew of strong punch, songs, and much tobacco smoke soon filled Candlish's tent with noise and steam. They insisted upon making Alured smoke for the first time in his life, and then, just as he was in the throes of sickness, all hands rushed out to bait a "spy." Some one had declared that the Smaitch (or native Maltee) who kept the canteen behind the camp, was in Russian pay. He had been observed to light up his canvas booth just before the sortie began. Of course this was a signal. Alured herded out with the others, bent upon pulling down the scoundrel's tent about his ears. In less than five minutes, the madcaps had broken into the canteen, and held the proprietor by the nape of the neck. Some were for hanging him on the spot; others, more lenient, dragged him out into the light of a lantern to scrutinize his features before he was handed over to the regimental guard. An abject wretch it was, who roared for mercy, and swore, in the best English, that he was a harmless London trader. As Alured looked on the man's face, it seemed to grow familiar. Yes; he recognised him. It was the footman who had insulted Lady Moynehan.

"Let him go!" cried Alured. "I know this man. I have met him before,—at home."

"Will you answer for his good behaviour?" asked some of the others with semi-drunken solemnity.

"Certainly."

"Then we'll let him go. But don't do it again; mind that. Next time we'll scrag you."

The wretch was only too glad to escape at

any price. Without one grateful glance towards Alured, his deliverer, he made one bound, the moment he was free, towards his tent. But he got back rather late in the day. It is wonderful how quickly old campaigners ascertain when liquor is to be had for the asking. Within a minute or two of the forcible entry into the spy's canteen, a crowd of soldiers had collected, despite the objections of the quarter-guard sentry, and had laid hands on everything. Porter barrels were rolled away, black wine drawn off in mess-tins from the cask, all the tobacco and most of the bottles were removed. To no purpose did the disconsolate proprietor seek to save his goods. The place was soon entirely gutted.

Next day the man had disappeared with the wreck of his belongings, and No. 3 of the General Orders, printed at Head-Quarters, contained a stringent injunction to repress all disorders in camp.

CHAPTER XIV.

BATTLE AND SIEGE.

"Why, soldiers, why,
Should we be melancholy, boys?
Why, soldiers, why,
Whose business 'tis to die."

YOUNG Frere was soon initiated into the ways of the place. First of all he had to get a mount, and in this Kensington stood his friend.

"You must have a nag," said Kensington.

"I'm afraid I can't afford—"

"Oh, it won't cost you much."

"Ah, but how much is that?"

"Just what you like to give,—a bottle of rum or a plug of tobacco."

"Is that the circulating medium here?"

"It is with my horse dealer. I'll send for him. It's a wonder he hasn't been here long before, for he pretends to be much attached to me, and calls himself my 'towney.' Perhaps he has been shot by the French sentries for marauding."

That evening, as they were dining off fried beef, a visitor was heard announcing himself outside.

"Is the captain in the tint beyant?"

"That's Driscoll," said Kensington; "we'll have him in."

Driscoll proved to be a Jack Tar belonging to the Naval Brigade. He appeared at the door of the tent, but would come no farther. On his back was some enormous burden, which it was impossible to make out quite distinctly in the dusk of the evening.

"What on earth have you got?" asked Kensington. "Drop it outside, and come in."

"Shure, captain, darling, it's a trifle I've brought for the new tint. They told me you'd dug it out and flured it, so I laid my hands on a nice little bit of matting to make ye a carpet for the flure. If I might make so bold, would you step out and look at it."

It was a mantlet. One of those great, bullet-proof, rope-woven screens, several inches thick, and at least six feet by four in dimensions. Driscoll must have stolen it from an embrasure in the trenches.

"Why where did you get this from?"

"Shure I found it, captain. It was a-lying about the camp."

"Now look here, my fine towney, you'll be tried by court-martial before you're many weeks older, unless you mend your ways. Do you know that these are Government stores you've been laying your hands upon? As sure as God made little apples, they'll scratch your back if they find you at these games."

Kensington's look and words were meant to be severe; but it was as much as he could do to restrain his laughter.

"And you want to implicate me as a receiver? You shall take it down to the trenches again,—this very night."

"I will, captain, I will, by dis cross," said Driscoll, crossing his two forefingers so as to make a rude effigy of a cross. "Shure I thought it'd plaze you."

"Well, come in and drink a glass of grog; but leave Government stores alone in future."

When the rum was finished, Kensington told Driscoll that Alured wanted a pony.

"A pony!" said Jack, as if he had heard of

such things, but was not quite certain whether they were fish, flesh, fowl, or good red-herring.

"Yes; a pony. Do you happen to know of any?"

"I saw one this very evening that'd suit him down to the ground."

"Not a Government one?"

"No, captain; shure he belongs to a friend of mine."

The pony was produced for inspection while Kensington was absent from camp. Alured liked the beast, and bought it for a song. Upon Kensington's return he recognised it as one of his own.

"Upon my word, that Driscoll's incorrigible," he said. But he insisted that Frere should keep the pony, which had been fairly bought. He himself was sold, but that was no matter. This was only a delicate way of making the boy a present.

Now that he was mounted, Alured was able to explore the country. Rides to Baidar Valley, to Kamiesch, and down to Balaclava, filled up the first few days; but he was not always clear of duty, and the Russians were kind enough to provide plenty of amusement for Frere soon after his arrival. It was the morning after Driscoll had sold him Kensington's pony, that the enemy attacked the French and Sardinians in the valley of the Tchernaya.

Alured was dressing, half in his own tent, half in that of a neighbour, when his attention was called to a lofty pillar of white smoke that rose straight into the sky at a distance of six or seven miles. There was a continuous rattling of musketry and banging of big guns in the same direction, so that the lad, imagining something extraordinary had happened, called to his servant to ask what it all meant.

"Which, sir?"

"That smoke, and all that."

"It's a battle, sir."

By this time others had collected: old Hicks, the major, and Kensington, McGuiness, and half a dozen more. News of this kind flies like wildfire through the camp. A staff officer comes galloping by. It is Underwood, the quarter-master general of the division; a light-hearted, jovial soldier, the life and soul of every bit of stirring work in these stirring times.

"Good-morning, Underwood," cries out Hicks. "Hold on a minute."

The other reins up.

"Morning. Fine morning," short and sharp. He was in a hurry. "Fine morning," he said, snuffing eagerly at the air. "Fine morning for a battle."

"What's going on?"

"They're hard at it down below there, Rooshies and Sardines—the other side of the Fedukhine heights."

"Where?"

"About Traktir Bridge. By-bye. I'm in a hurry—going to head-quarters."

The battle was raging fiercely, and almost as fiercely beat the young blood in Alured's heart.

"Oh, Kensington, let's go and see it."

"With all my heart."

The ponies were ordered, and in less than ten minutes they were in their saddles.

"Stop, stop!" cried Kensington to Alured, who was cantering on far ahead.

"What's the matter?"

"There goes the assembly."

True enough. The bugles of every regiment in the division were blowing away as if they were the last trumpets.

"What a nuisance! We must turn back, I suppose."

They were not much too soon, for they found the 145th fallen in on parade. In another minute they marched to the divisional parade ground, and there remained until night, cooped up among the tents, without even a glimpse of the battle in progress about Traktir Bridge. Such is the fighting men's luck: either in the thick of the smoke and din, quite lost to all that is passing around them, or in reserve behind a hill, or far away waiting on the divisional parade for orders to march. The common men and the regimental officers see but little of the game. All the front seats in the stalls are reserved for the newspaper correspondents and the staff. In action, the world of a subaltern like Alured Frere is narrowed indeed, and his view does not extend much beyond the pouches of the men just in front.

Alured's experiences of a battle-field were reserved till the following day, when, released from confinement to camp, he got leave to ride over the ground at Traktir Bridge. The sight was somewhat appalling. The carnage of the fight was evident around, in the hideous shapeless masses that lay about, bodies heaped one above another in an undistinguishable tangle—arms, legs, and heads, twisted in and out with agonized contortions, as if thus, writhing and in torture, the breath of life had been spent at last. Alured and his companion lingered about the spots where the battle had raged most fiercely, and where the dead lay thick. One, a Zouave, who seemed stooping to tie his shoe, knelt a little apart. Alured went up and touched him. The body toppled over: the man had been shot through the heart. And yet there was a strange fascination in this utter desolation of death. It was something to be remembered for years. Already under the burning sun of the south, the corpses were changing colour. And all alike, friend and foe, as they gazed up with lack-lustre eyes at the brazen sky, were turning black in the face.

"My God, how awful!" said Frere, almost involuntarily.

"You ought not to stay here. Come away," answered Kensington, taking him by the arm.

"Stay. There—there! I saw a leg move," shouted Alured suddenly, in a frenzy almost, pointing to a matted mass of corpses at his feet.

"Nonsense. Come away."

"I did, I swear. There it is again; the same man too. He is moving his arm now. Let us help him out."

They tore away furiously at the superincumbent carcases, throwing them to right and left; digging furiously like terrier dogs in this great mound of mortality. Presently they reached the man, who was yet alive, and thanked them with his eyes as they dragged him forth. It was in vain that he essayed to speak—a bullet had passed through his lungs. He could find no voice, but there was a horrid gurgling in his throat repeated at each attempt at respiration. Kensington tried to place the poor wretch, a Sardinian trooper, as easily as he could, while Frere ran off to fetch up a doctor who was at work at the other end of the field. It was no avail; the hurt was mortal. There was nothing for it but to lay the wounded man out, and leave him to die. But neither of those young fellows could leave the spot until the death-rattle and the last terrible throe proved that life was indeed extinct.

But it soon came to be Alured's turn for the trenches. This time he went down on duty, and did not feel at all ashamed of himself, until they passed a picquet of Frenchmen, who turned out, one and all, to look and laugh at *ce petit enfant.* His own men had christened him "the baby" long before this, and it was rather a sore subject. Inwardly he had resolved to show them, if he got a chance, that he was no baby. But everything was so new and strange out here. Hardly had the men of the 145th settled themselves down in the trench after their arrival at the second parallel, when a voice cried out,—

"The captain in command of the 145th covering party?"

It was the field officer on duty for the left attack.

"Yes, sir; here."

"You are to send a party of fifty men and an officer back to the first parallel—is that where they are to go?" he inquired of an engineer standing by.

"To the first parallel, and fetch up a—a—a Gibraltar gyn that is lying there."

"Gibraltar gyn. Very good, sir. Mr. Frere, you must go; take fifty, the first fifty you can fall in, and be off."

The men hated "fatigue" work, as it was extra labour, and Alured had some trouble in getting his fifty together. But at length he marched the party away, their comrades crying out as they left, " Right face; follow the sapper"—a piece of thread-bare Crimean chaff for which half a hundred explanations were given. It was generally supposed that a sapper who headed a party thus entrusted to his guidance, had returned with only one man out of the dozen or more that started. The rest had "gone under."

But there was no sapper this time; and when Alured had groped his way back to the first parallel, he was rather at a loss where to find his Gibraltar gyn. Besides, what was a Gibraltar gyn? Was it something to drink? he asked his sergeant, and his sergeant, licking his lips, said he hoped it was. They wandered about, Frere and his fifty men, till they were a nuisance to every one in Greenhill Trench.

"Who on earth are you," said a "gunner" officer, "and what is it you want?"

"Some 'gin,' or something."

"You're a green hand. It's that Gibraltar gyn I suppose. Here, Sergeant Atkins, hand over that gyn to this party."

The object of Alured's search proved to be something like a gallows or guillotine frame. But he was glad to get it, and asked no questions. The gyn was taken to pieces, and carried to the front, where they were getting rather impatient.

"You've been a confounded long time," said the officer in charge rather sharply to Alured; "we shall never get done before daylight, I'm afraid."

They were placing a sea-service mortar in a new battery. The gunners of the field battery, who, with their horses, had brought the piece down to the trench, remained to help. So did Alured's men, as it was a heavy job. All were soon hard at work. The night was "quiet," but guns were fired at regular intervals on both sides; sometimes shot and sometimes shell. It chanced that one of these was directed at the spot where the men, round Alured, were working at the mortar; and suddenly there rose a cry among them of "Shell, shell!" The mere words were sufficient to strike every one dumb. Sure enough amid the death-like silence that prevailed, the peculiar creaking, sing-song of the approaching projectile was plainly audible.

It comes closer, closer, closer. Suspense; breathless suspense; and then a murmur bursts forth from this silent band thus momentarily expecting death, a sort of hoarse groan, the voice of their tense-strung feelings. What thoughts are afloat I wonder among that handful of human beings, standing, for all they know, upon the brink of an open grave? Are there any who employ the brief instant on thoughts of repentance; any who view at that awful moment in their mind's eye the happy home, far away, with its dear ones, never, perhaps, to be met with again on earth? It is said that a drowning man sees at the acme of his danger the past actions of his life move like a rapid panorama before him. The men who stood with Alured Frere must needs make haste. Quick—the fatal moment is advancing rapidly as thought; already a harsh hissing, rushing, whistling sound has replaced the soft creaking of the distant shell; the light of its fuse is now in sight above the trench, like a falling star, slowly descending through the dark purple vault.

Whish, whish, whist; sh—sht, *st. thud.*

"It's down! Where?"

"Short! short! It has fallen outside the trench!" some one cries out with joyful voice.

The next moment his statement is confirmed, as with violent explosion, uprooting as it seems, all the ground about them, the fragments are blown into the sky. Another second, the murderous shower of iron raindrops has fallen, and no one is hurt. All is over.

"Turn to, men!" the officer in command cries out sharply.

There is no time for sentiment. Danger for the present is past; there must be no romantic stock-taking of the agony endured through those moments of excruciating suspense. Onward! Leave all the rest behind; as the drums and fifes strike up a lively air returning from the grave of a comrade, newly filled.

With nights like this Alured interspersed others more dangerous, spending hours under a heavy fire, and risking his life often. Foolhardiness came to be a matter of competition between him and his companions. It was an exciting game, to try who would stand longest above the trench, and brave the most shots; to go across the "open," and touch that gunner's body who was killed there that morning; to sneak out at night beyond our line and beard the Russian sentries in their shelter pits. In one of these madcap escapades, one bullet pierced Alured's coat, and another took his hat off. The jagged hole in his jacket, with the long irregular tear which the shot had made, were like trophies, and our hero began to take rank as one who had really smelt powder.

Meanwhile the siege dragged itself; but the end was near at hand. Another attack was imminent. Unmistakable warnings were current. The commander-in-chief had been seen reconnoitring from Cathcart's Hill alone, all one afternoon. Woolbags to fill the ditch of the Redan were being made at the engineer park. There had been a council of war at headquarters. The attack was to come off to-morrow, to-morrow, and to-morrow, till the day did dawn at length. Alured, who had spent the previous night on duty in the trenches, saw it all, in the face of a tornado, a perfect whirlwind of dust, from the left attack. The assailants, like a thin black line—Rifles first—ran out from the flying sap, across the open to the Redan. How few they seemed! and yet of these, half are swept away by the first fire of the enemy's guns. More follow. The *chevaux de frises* gained, the woolbags are thrown down into the ditch; the great earthen mound of the Redan is scaled. At the top, Greeks meet Greek; and all scramble back together. All round, the air is hideous with the roar of guns, great and small; smoke rises in clouds. Moments, minutes, hours of anxious suspense for those who watch from without, and wait. Within the womb of the Redan all is mystery; but that the fighting is sharp, is proved by the unceasing fire, the occasional sight of a body blown into the air, of men mortally stricken, who drop back over the slope to fall and die. "Why don't they send on more men!" cry, almost in frenzied excitement, those who, under a heavy fire themselves, stand round Alured in the left attack. The trenches are quite crammed with troops. They are to be seen plainly: Highlanders, a whole division from Kamara; Guards, Marines not long landed, and still fresh and unworn by the hardships or losses of the campaign. What is Simpson about? Why does he hesitate? If he would only let them loose,—over the trench and on. But the time wears away. The Fourth Division is there too; and the Third is at the Park. Nothing is wanted but the word to advance.

But no word is given. The handful that went out has got to do it all.

The task is clearly beyond their strength, and there can be none of them left by this time—stay, yes; a few; for see, they are retreating! Englishmen retreating, falling back, withered, crestfallen, unsuccessful.

A feeling of deep gloom settles on those in the left attack, who have had no share in the fight, and are too far distant to get intelligence of what has passed. That the assault has again failed at the Redan, they have the evidence of their own eyes. But what is to be the next move? Will not fresh storming parties be organized without delay? Rumour and counter rumour fly like wildfire. Four companies of the 145th were in the action. The colonel is killed, and the adjutant, they say. The enemy, flushed with success, is about to make a combined sortie all along their line; while Liprandi, advancing from the Tchernaya Valley, storms the Fedhukhine Heights. Then it becomes known that the Malakoff has been captured—and why not the Redan?

"It was never meant to be taken; the attack was a feint to draw attention from the Malakoff."

"Then the French have all the glory; ours is the shame."

Evening now draws on. Alured, with McGuiness is sent to the advanced trenches; and sentries are once more posted, and the night is passed anxiously awaiting a Russian onslaught. Just before dawn, as they lie extended on the ground within the trench, worn out and tired, their backs are nearly broken by a violent convulsion of the earth beneath them. A terrible roar follows. "A mine! a mine! They will advance under cover of this." The men stand to their arms silently, expecting the worst.

The light grows stronger; but it is garish, sickly, artificial, as if the dawn broke sick at heart at all the carnage it must see at waking. Is it really day-break; or are the heavens on fire?

No. Sebastopol is in flames; the enemy has evacuated the place, leaving smoking ruins, forts crumbled into dust,—an empty shell, void of life or value to its jaded captors.

CHAPTER XV.

A CHANCE SHOT.

"What, sighing? fie!
Drink on; drown fear; be jolly, boys;
'Tis he, you, or I."

AFTER the fall of Sebastopol there was a lull in hostilities. But rumour, within a week, was busy inventing fresh outlets for the allied arms. It was asserted, for instance, that the whole of our forces were to embark forthwith for Asia, to raise the siege of Kars. For this purpose the fleet had been ordered to rendezvous at Kamiesch. Then it became known that a combined assault was meditated upon the Mackenzie Heights, beyond the Tchernaya, striking thus at Batchiserai and Simpheropol in the interior. After which, it was probable that the armies would march upon Moscow or St. Petersburgh, time, and the coming winter being naturally neither object nor obstacle. There was plenty of tall talk about the camps, till September had passed without a move beyond some trifling naval operations in the Sea of Azof. It became evident then that nothing much would be attempted that year, and our brave soldiers, like Cæsar's legions in Gaul, went into winter quarters. Those who disliked their tents built huts, taught by the experience of the past to guard against the hardships of the coming winter. All ranks tried to make themselves comfortable. The troops were flush of cash, thanks to their increased pay, and spent it like men, as who should say "See how we soldiers live! Sometimes better, and never worse." Tobacco was a drug in the camp; grog flowed in streams; biscuit, as a ration, despised for the fresh soft bread sold daily by the Maltee hawkers. In this respect there was a marked difference between the English and French armies. As supplies poured in to the former, the latter became more and more straitened. There was hardly a regiment in the British encampment but had a strong *clientèle* of hungry French pensioners, who were fed after meals with what was left. Every morning a lean *piou-piou* came past Alured's tent, following a trail of crumbs laid by the men of Alured's company, to show where the buried heap of biscuits was concealed. And if the English soldiers fared so well, the officers were not much worse off. Had there been a pack or two of hounds in the neighbourhood, or more shooting than the few snipe down in the Tchernaya marsh, they would have been quite contented. As it was every effort was made to supply the loss. Dogs were hunted instead of foxes, paper chases organized on the wildest principles of "larking across country." Sometimes a sportsman, with memories of moor or Norfolk strong upon him, dropped down upon the snipe, and wiped the eye of the French and Sardinians, who stalked their bird in full regimentals, booted and spurred, with sword girded on to despatch the winged. Steeple chases and flat races were announced for a coming day; amateur theatricals and glee clubs filled up the evenings; while rather under the rose, those who suffered most from ennui developed a strong taste for gambling at "unlimited loo."

In all these sports the 145th were not behind-hand; and it might have fallen to our hero's fate to graduate as a gambler or a light weight jock, had not his regiment got the route one fine morning for Kamiesch. The brigade to which it belonged was to form part of a secret expedition in the northernmost regions of the Black Sea.

It was not till a week had been spent on board ship, sailing off the coast of the Crimea, or anchored in front of Odessa till its peaceful inhabitants were half frantic with terror, that the expeditionary force found that their mark was Kinburn, a fort unimportant in itself, but with that of Otchakoff, opposite, closing the mouth of the river Bug, the high road to Nicholaieff and Kherson.

The reduction of Kinburn was after all but an inglorious achievement for the combined fleets of England and France. It was scarcely more than a naval parade; and the troops destined to co-operate in this great enterprise hardly fired a shot. Bazaine, later conqueror in Mexico, but also commander-in-chief in Metz, led the French, Spencer the English, contingent.

A long low spit of land, a sand-bank eaten

into by the aggressive tide, treeless, lonely, and deserted, with patches here and there of a thin vegetation,—such was Kinburn, viewed from the pontoons that conveyed the invading army through the long shallows to shore. Theirs were keen eyes which magnified the long-legged sea-birds upon the beach into an enemy's sharpshooters; an imagination very vivid was required to make columns of troops out of the sand-dunes. There was no opposition to the landing, no enemies to overcome greater than hunger and ennui. The latter was inevitable except for sand-crabs or blow-flies; the former might have been avoided by a proper husbanding of the salt provisions each officer and man was ordered to carry. Indeed the chance of starvation stared all in the face; and a strict search among the deserted hovels that did duty for villages brought nothing to light but vats full of pickled gherkins floating fish-like in a sea of brine. These were but the leavings of the Turcos, who, light-fingered foragers, had swept like locusts across the land.

In munching biscuits, digging sand-pits as shelter, harvesting the wild reeds for bedding, day followed day, till Grimes,—who had joined his master, not from devotion, but because the doctor thought he would be the better for a little campaigning,—declared he'd rather have a month in the *provost* cells.

"There's stones there to break at any rate," said Grimes. "Divil a pebble on this big sairey."

"There's no Saireys nor Mary's nuther in Rooshia, you great omahdawn," cried a comrade, in correction.

"Go 'long wid ye. I call to mind when I was in the regimental school, I saw that sairey was furrin for sand, and these Rooshie women are all sandy, that's why they christen them Sairey's."

Grimes was a little out of date. The prestige he enjoyed as an old soldier was gone in the presence of veteran campaigners who had been at Alma and the Redan, while he had never seen a shot fired. It kept him on the stretch to be even with his comrades. He talked continually of the days when the regiment lay at "Moulmain," and "Bellary." They capped his stories with descriptions of hand-to-hand fights at Inkerman. They told him of Dooley the recruit, that flung away his rifle just before the last attack, and called for his mother, and how the general had sent for Dooley, and said, "You think you belong to your mother, do you? You belong to your country, sir,—to be shot, or otherwise disposed of." Upon which Grimes swore Dooley was a disgrace to the regiment, and said that at Tounghoo there were "doolies" and "coolies" too.

"It's like the riffraff that 'lists these days," Grimes went on. "With your doolies. Shure, when I was a recruit at drill, I had a real lord for a rear rank man."

"Not you!"

"By this cross. No less. Own son to the divil do I know who. And his father came and bought him out one morning as we stood upon parade. Driving on the square in a coach and four."

"Was that the last of him?"

"Not at all. He was that fond of us, he gave his father the slip, and re-enlisted. A mighty big drink we had over his second bounty. There was many lost their stripes over that."

"And what became of his lordship?"

"He died at Moulmain of the horrors. Drought did it. He was such a thirsty chap."

Grimes was interrupted by his master's voice.

Alured was for outlying picquet that night with his company, condemned to keep watch through the long hours, and protect the rest from surprise. It was just possible that the enemy might make an effort to relieve the fort of Kinburn, dropping down in force from Nicholaieff, where they had a large garrison, to drive the besiegers into the sea. Across the isthmus, therefore, was drawn a chain of posts, strong enough to hold in check any attack until it was fully developed, and until the main body behind had time to stand to its arms. Far in front of the outposts double sentries patrolled right, left, and forward, listening sometimes with ear to earth, at others getting low down into the hollows, so as to bring the ground in front against the sky-line.

The party to which Alured belonged was

right across the main road from Nicholaieff, and held the key of the position. A little to the front lay a few hovels,—half village, half overgrown homestead,—quite deserted now, but capable of giving cover to the *éclaireurs* of an advancing enemy. Taking with him an escort of a dozen men, Alured visited this place more than once during the night, but found all quiet. In this and in visiting the line of sentries the time passed, till, towards morning, our hero threw himself upon the sand, tired out, meaning to have forty winks, waking up first his sergeant to take his place on the look-out.

Campaigners may be said to have got the better of conscience, sleep comes to them so easily. Not even the memory of atrocious crimes could keep a man awake whose day had been spent on the line of march and his evening by the bivouac fire. For him the cold ground is a softer bed than springs or feathers could provide, and his head sinks into the sand as if it were a luxurious pillow. Alured was soon sound asleep; next minute, as it seemed, he was awakened by a shot.

"A shot fired in front!" The picquet stood

to its arms; Alured ran to place himself at the head of his men, and sent back to give the alarm.

A second shot!

A third!

The sentries had been ordered not to fire, but to fall back at once upon their supporters. It was evident they could not restrain themselves. The enemy must be quite close upon them. In another minute Alured expected to be engaged.

With nerves strung tight, yet with beating anxious heart he awaited attack. Five minutes passed. No more firing in front, no Cossacks. The sentries had not even fallen back! Alured was on the point of sending out a strong patrol to reconnoitre his front, when he seemed to observe in the scant, dim light, something moving towards him. A body, lightish in colour (the Russians he knew wore grey) creeping with slow cautious steps up to where he and his picquet stood. Could the enemy have forced their way unobserved through the line of sentries? A terrible moment this. Should he receive them with a volley? No; perhaps he had better reserve his fire to the last. Nearer and nearer came his strange mysterious assailant; faster and faster beat his heart; then all at once it went,—snap!

Another shot, this time close under their noses.

Then a voice, a well-known voice, crying out in joyful accents :—

"I've kilt him; I've kilt him. Hurrah, boys! he's as dead as mutton."

Rushing forward, Alured and his men found Grimes astride of a cow!

"What's the meaning of this?" asked his master sternly. "What have you been up to? The whole force is under arms by this time. Make a prisoner of him," he went on to the sergeant. "I'll teach you to play the fool. Send him back to the regiment with an escort."

"And me cow, sir?" said Grimes, with a groan. "Sorrow a taste of fresh meat these weeks, and I saw the devilish beast go by. How could I help it?"

By this time the field officer on duty for the night came up (he was one of the majors of the 145th) to inquire into the cause of disturbance. Alured explained.

"You old rascal!" said the major, with a laugh; "you must take the consequences of this. March him into the quarter-guard. But, Mr. Frere," in a lower tone, "take care of the cow. It won't go a great way among the whole force, but there's enough to give all the men of our regiment a ration a-piece to-morrow. I think we'd better say nothing about this. Between ourselves, it would be better to hush the whole thing up. Sentries got excited,—fired without necessity,—and so forth." And Grimes was dealt very leniently with, for in his way he was a benefactor to his fellow-men. The jaws that chewed the tough fresh beef next day, in the 145th camp, had their work cut out for them; but the men were not too busy to forget a word of praise for the valiant sportsman who had killed the cow.

In this bloodless Kinburn campaign, Grimes' rifle was, with one exception, the only weapon discharged by the 145th. Alured Frere's revolver was the other.

The fort itself fell without striking a blow.

It was hammered to pieces in half an hour by the murderous cannonade of the combined fleets, and all was over. But before the troops were re-embarked, the generals in command resolved to make a reconnaissance in force. Two strong columns marched inland for a couple of days, presumably to stretch their legs, and see the country. A closer inspection developed nothing but sand, and more sand. Sometimes a few trees; here and there a little sparse brushwood; at one or two places a group of huts, now empty, which once had done duty as a village. Near one of these, on the evening of the first day, the 145th bivouacked. The march had been long and dreary, the allowance of rations limited, and Alured with his friend, Kensington, lay down in a hastily erected sand hovel, roofed with a few reeds, open at one end, where a scanty fire was kept up, to growl themselves to sleep. During the night a drizzling rain fell without intermission, and made its way almost at once through their threadbare shelter. Soon after dawn the whole camp, weary of the comfortless night, was astir. Frere and his captain woke like the rest, saddened and sulky, to pick the sand out of their gummy eyes, and swear at Grimes for not relighting the fire. As they sat side by side, in their miserable den, chilled in every bone, they thought of home, and dry clothes, and a comfortable breakfast.

"What a night!" said Kensington. "I'd as soon have slept in a gutter."

"Do you remember 'Margery Daw,' who sold her bed and laid upon straw? I wish we'd had some straw last night. I'm in a pool of water. It'll play the mischief, this wet, with our swords and things."

"And the revolvers. Where's yours, Boy Frere?"

Alured hunted, and found it half soaked with the rain, and rusting already.

"You'd better clean it, and put it to rights. We might have a brush with the Rooshies by-and-by. I shall rub up mine."

"Yes, I would," said Alured, with a laugh; "it wants it."

There was a good deal of rivalry about the respective merits of their weapons.

"It's worth a dozen of yours. You boys

who've just come out, think everything must be brand new to be of use."

" Mine must be more use than that old rattle-trap of yours. Why the spring's got all clogged with sand."

" The spring works easy enough. Look."

" Let me try."

" No; try your own."

" Talk about springs—ah !"

A report, a wild scared shout from a group standing by, one short groan from Alured, and the deed was done.

" Good heavens !" cried Kensington. " What has happened ? What are those fellows staring at. Did any one fall. You have hit some one."

"Yes," said Alured, faintly; " I've hit—myself."

There was a little hole in his trowsers just above the knee. The cloth was torn, and a small thin wisp of smoke curled up from the spot where the bullet had entered. Alured Frere had shot himself in the leg.

A minute more, and the news flew through the camp. The regimental doctors came to probe the wound, while Kensington stood by holding poor Alured's hand, and Grimes administered doses of brandy. Friends (and among those, already, in the few months that he had served, the baby-faced boy counted all the regiment) waited anxiously for the verdict. Was there any immediate danger. No, thank Heaven, no immediate danger. And then, in a whisper, the surgeon told the colonel that he feared it would be necessary to amputate the leg.

"Not here, surely? We're on the march, and might be attacked any moment. There is no field hospital."

"No, not here, of course. We'll send him back to the coast. The *Bountiful* is there, you know, sir, the hospital ship. He'll do on a small litter. His servant with him, and Townshend, the assistant-surgeon, to see him on board."

Kensington pressed Alured's hand as they parted.

"It was all my fault! If I'd never said anything about those cursed revolvers——"

"No, no, no; it was my own."

The journey tried our hero's courage. Although late in the year, the October sun beat down fiercely on his poor feverish face, and the wound, self-inflicted, ached and pained him horribly. Looking back upon it in after-days, Alured seemed, in that day's march, to have suffered the agony of a lifetime. By the time they lifted him into a boat he was speechless. Townshend began to be alarmed, and Grimes was in tears.

Painted in black upon a white square, the *Bountiful* bore upon her bows the numerals 337, her number in the transport service. She was a sailing ship; a large, commodious East Indiaman, fitted up as a floating hospital, with sick bays clean and airy, swinging cots, a captain of the orderlies, a staff of doctors, and a cargo of medicines and surgical instruments. Balaclava Harbour was her home, but they had sent her up in tow to Kinburn to provide for any casualties that might occur in the campaign. Beyond a few Russians injured in the bombardment, so far there had been no demand upon the *Bountiful's* accommodation, and those who formed her cabin company, finding time heavy upon their hands, fought as only men of the same profession can, or, being already far advanced towards dyspepsia from over-feeding without exercise, abused the table kept on board.

One voice in particular was heard above all the din, louder in tone and fiercer in invective than all the rest—Starkie's.

From morning till night Starkie swore at everything in the ship. At early dawn he cursed the seamen holystoning the deck over head; next the steward, who would not give him a brandy and soda before breakfast; then the food set in front of him. By-and-by he quarrelled with his assistants because they could not play whist as well as himself, and wished to heaven they'd send him some work from shore, if it was only to save him from his companions,—a case of cholera or two, or some good gunshot wounds. But the purser was his chief enemy. "I'd like to prescribe for you, Mr. Crouch," Starkie would say to him with a fiendish grin. "If you would only lay up now, and call me in, I'd pay you off for the filth you've made me eat on board your bountiful ship. I'd let you know what filth tasted like."

They were in the middle of dinner when the boat containing Alured and his attendants came alongside. Starkie was making a running commentary on the bill of fare in his loudest tones, calling the soup dish-water, and asking for fish. "No fish? with the sea all round us. Veal cutlets! pah! 'Slink' veal out of a tin. Boiled beef; drowned horse. Fresh pork; I like that! Fresh from the pickle-tub. Get me some cold meat, steward; some cold meat and pickles. Pickles; you know what I mean; piccalilli, or Captain White, or Black, or gunner's delight, or mumbo jumbo,—anything just to make the stuff go down."

Then some one coming down into the cabin, said an officer had been brought on board badly wounded.

"What's that?" roared Starkie. "Fighting begun, eh?"

"It's an officer of the 145th—" but before Starkie could hear more, Grimes appeared with a scared face, and went up to him.

"Shure I heard your voice, doctor, darling.

I hope ye'll remember the dipot, and old times. There's bad luck come on us," said the old soldier, half breaking down.

"What are you whimpering at, you great ass?" cried Starkie.

"My boy! oh, my boy!"

"What boy? You're not a father, are you? I thought you were a miserable old bachelor like myself."

"No, doctor; shure, sir, it's me master that's a boy I mean."

"What, master?" asked Starkie, rising to interest at once.

"Little Mr. Frere, sir. He's badly hot— hot in the leg, sir. Iss, sir; iss, sir," faltered Grimes, in snuffling accents.

"Where was the fighting?" asked Starkie.

"There was no fighting at all, sir. He hot himself in the leg, sir; iss, sir; iss, sir."

Starkie, without waiting for more, rushed on deck. They had already taken Alured below, and he was in his cot, looking very pale and white, by the time that Starkie found him. Townshend, with an anxious face, sat by his side.

"Poor boy!" said the old doctor, in such a strange soft voice that it might have come from some other man. "Poor little chap. I am sorry to see this. But we'll put you right, never fear. You know me, don't you?"

Alured's answer was a faint flush, of pleasure probably at meeting with his former friend; but he could not speak.

Townshend took Starkie aside, and told him the whole story.

"We're afraid the leg will have to come off."

"Are you to wait with us?" Starkie asked.

"No; they want me back with the regiment."

"Then I can take the case into my own hands. This little chap is an old friend of mine; and his leg shall be saved, if I can do it."

Never had wounded man nurse so tender and attentive. Starkie forsook everything for Alured Frere. It was the wonder of the whole ship. He scarcely left the lad's bedside; and when there, was as gentle and quiet as a woman, modulating his rough voice to speak in whispers, and treading with noiseless step as he moved across the sick bay. This godless, cross-grained, old reprobate seemed suddenly transformed. The dangerous illness of this boy, to whom he had taken such a strange liking, woke in him all those better feelings which had long been buried beneath the crust of his dried-up heart.

His devotion met with its reward. After some days the ball was extracted. Fever followed; a prostrating fever that retarded the healing of the wound. Alured was moved to Balaclava; thence to Scutari; and at last to England, reaching Scaggleton just twelve months after his departure from home.

Starkie accompanied him.

"I owe it all to him, mother," said our hero, pointing to the doctor, who stood somewhat apart from the family group, as they fondled and caressed the dear one who had come back, as it were, from the grave. "He saved my life."

"May the great God bless you, Doctor Starkie," said Mrs. Frere, going up to him, with solemn face and streaming eyes, and taking his big brown hands into hers, she kissed them. "You have saved my life, too, I think."

Starkie, for the first time in his life, felt almost unmanned. He blushed even, and could say nothing at first; but I doubt whether for years and years he had known any such emotion of pure pleasure as swelled his heart at that moment.

"Don't, ma'am; don't speak about it," said Starkie at length, in a husky voice.

Nor were the others behindhand in their gratitude and thanks. Starkie had never been made so much of before. He was more a hero, if it were possible, than Alured himself.

The winter was now nearly past, and the war was at an end. The Crimean army, broken up, passed in driblets to various stations at home and abroad. And by the summer, Alured was able to rejoin his regiment, perfectly restored to health and strength.

END OF VOL. I.

65, Cornhill, and 12, Paternoster Row,
London, *December*, 1872.

A CATALOGUE OF BOOKS,

PUBLISHED BY

HENRY S. KING & CO.

Messrs. HENRY S. KING & CO. *have the pleasure to announce that in future the following Periodicals will be published by them.*

I.

On the 1st January, 1873, *will be published*, NUMBER I. OF

THE DAY OF REST.

PRICE ONE PENNY A WEEK.

In Large Folio Size. Illustrated by the Best Artists.

AN INTRODUCTORY CHRISTMAS NUMBER
Will be published on the 21st December. Price **ONE PENNY.**
SPLENDIDLY ILLUSTRATED.

II.

THE CONTEMPORARY REVIEW. Theological, Literary, and Social. Price 2s. 6d. Monthly.

[*A New Volume began December*, 1872.

III.

THE SAINT PAUL'S MAGAZINE. Light and Choice. Price 1s. Monthly.

[*A New Volume begins January*, 1873.

IV.

GOOD THINGS for the Young of all Ages. Edited by GEORGE MACDONALD, and Illustrated by the best Artists. Price 6d. Monthly.

[*A New Volume began November*, 1872.

Preparing for Publication.

I.
LOMBARD STREET. A description of the Money Market. By WALTER BAGEHOT. Author of "The English Constitution," "Physics and Politics," &c. Large crown 8vo. [*Shortly.*

II.
THE YOUNG LIFE EQUIPPING ITSELF FOR GOD'S SERVICE. Being four Sermons preached before the University of Cambridge in November, 1872. By the Rev. J. C. VAUGHAN, D.D., Master of the Temple. [*Immediately.*

MR. EDWARD JENKINS'S WORKS.

I.
A CHRISTMAS COUNTRY CAROL,
By the Author of "Ginx's Baby."
NOW READY, PRICE ONE SHILLING.

LITTLE HODGE. By EDWARD JENKINS, Author of "Ginx's Baby." [*Just Ready.*

New Editions.

II.
GINX'S BABY: His Birth and other Misfortunes.
[*Twenty-ninth Edition in a few days.*

III.
LORD BANTAM. [*Sixth Edition in a few days.*

A New Work.

IV.
LUTCHMEE AND DILLOO. A Study of West Indian Life. [*In January.*

I.
MEMOIR AND LETTERS OF SARA COLERIDGE. With Portrait. Two vols., crown 8vo.

65, *Cornhill, and* 12, *Paternoster Row, London.*

II.

A WINTER IN MOROCCO. By AMELIA PERRIER, Author of "A Good Match." Illustrated.

III.

ESSAYS BY WILLIAM GODWIN, Author of "Political Justice," &c. Now first collected. One vol., crown 8vo.

IV.

ARABIC STORIES AND LEGENDS. Translated from the Originals by Mrs. GODFREY CLERK.

V.

PERSIAN LEGENDS AND STORIES IN ENGLISH VERSE. Translated by Lieut. NORTON POWLETT, R.A. [*In Dec.*

VI.

EGYPT AS IT IS. By Herr H. STEPHAN, the German Postmaster-General. With a new Map of the Country.

VII.

BRESSANT. A ROMANCE. By JULIAN HAWTHORNE, son of the late Nathaniel Hawthorne. Two vols., crown 8vo.

VIII.

A splendidly Illustrated Edition of
WILLIAM CULLEN BRYANT'S POEMS. Collected and arranged by the Author. [*In Dec.*

IX.

A Pocket Edition of
WILLIAM CULLEN BRYANT'S POEMS. Beautifully printed. [*In Dec.*

X.

THE GREAT DUTCH ADMIRALS. By JACOB DE LIEFDE. Illustrated. [*In Dec.*

XI.

GOETHE'S FAUST. A New Translation. By the Rev. C. K. PAUL. Crown 8vo. [*Just ready.*

65, *Cornhill, and* 12, *Paternoster Row, London.*

XII.

LIFE: Conferences delivered at Toulouse. By the Rev. PÈRE LACORDAIRE, of the order of Friar Preachers. Translated from the French, with the Author's permission, by a Tertiary of the same order. Crown 8vo. [*Just ready.*

XIII.

FIELD AND FOREST RAMBLES OF A NATURALIST IN NEW BRUNSWICK. By Dr. A. LEITH ADAMS, F.R.S., &c. Demy 8vo. Illustrated. [*Just ready.*

XIV.

THE TASMANIAN LILY. By JAMES BONWICK. [*Shortly.*

XV.

IMPERIAL GERMANY. By FREDERIC MARTIN. Author of "The Statesman's Year-Book," etc.

XVI.

PANDURANG HARI. A Tale of Mahratta Life, sixty years ago. Edited, from the edition of 1826, by Sir HENRY BARTLE E. FRERE, G.C.S.I., K.C.B.

XVII.

REMINISCENCES OF TRAVANCORE. By the Rev. RICHARD COLLINS. Illustrated.

XVIII.

AN ARABIC AND ENGLISH DICTIONARY OF THE KORAN By Major J. PENRICE. Post 4to.

Works Just Published.

I.
BOKHARA: ITS HISTORY AND CONQUEST. By Professor ARMINIUS VAMBERY, of the University of Pesth. Author of "Travels in Central Asia," etc. Demy 8vo. Price 18s.
[*Ready.*

II.
Now Ready, Price Sixpence.
LONDON MIXTURE,
The CHRISTMAS NUMBER of "GOOD THINGS."
By the Author of "Lilliput Levee," the Author of "The Boys of Axleford," and the Author of "King George's Middy."
Illustrated by ARTHUR HUGHES, ERNEST GRISET, and W. J. WIEGAND.

III.
THE PELICAN PAPERS. Reminiscences and Remains of a Dweller in the Wilderness. By JAMES A. NOBLE. Crown 8vo, 6s.

IV.
WORDS AND WORKS IN A LONDON PARISH. Edited by the Rev. C. ANDERSON, M.A. Demy 8vo. Price 6s.

V.
PHYSICS AND POLITICS; or, Thoughts on the Application of the Principles of "Natural Selection" and "Inheritance" to Political Society. By WALTER BAGEHOT. Crown 8vo. 4s
Being Vol. II. of The International Scientific Series.

VI.
A MEMOIR OF NATHANIEL HAWTHORNE, with Stories now first Published in this Country. By H. A. PAGE. Large post 8vo. 7s. 6d.

65, Cornhill, and 12, Paternoster Row, London.

VII.
STREAMS FROM HIDDEN SOURCES. By B. MONTGOMERIE RANKING. Crown 8vo. 6s.

THE SEVEN STREAMS ARE:

Cupid and Psyche.	Sir Urre of Hungary.
The Life of St. Eustace.	Isabella; or, The Pot of Basil.
Alexander and Lodowick.	The Marriage of Belphegor.

Fulgencius.

"Out of all old lore I have chosen seven books as setting forth seven following stages of time, and from each of these have taken what seemed to me the best thing, so that any man may judge, and if it please him trace it to its source."—*Extract from Preface.*

VIII.
REPUBLICAN SUPERSTITIONS. Illustrated by the political history of the United States. Including a correspondence with M. Louis Blanc. By MONCURE D. CONWAY. Crown 8vo. 5s.

IX.
THE ENGLISH CONSTITUTION. By WALTER BAGEHOT A New Edition, revised and corrected, with an Introductory Dissertation on recent changes and events. Crown 8vo, 7s. 6d.

X.
MEMORIES OF VILLIERSTOWN. By C. S. J. Crown 8vo. With Frontispiece. 5s.

XI.
CABINET PORTRAITS. Sketches of Statesmen. By T. WEMYSS REID. One Vol., Crown 8vo., 7s. 6d.

Mr. Gladstone.	Mr. Wilson-Patten.	Marquis of Salisbury.
Mr. Disraeli.	The Earl of Carnarvon.	Duke of Richmond.
The Earl of Derby.	Earl Russell.	Lord Westbury.
Mr. Lowe.	Lord John Manners.	Mr. Forster.
Mr. Hardy.	Mr. Cardwell.	Mr. Newdegate.
Mr. Bright.	Lord Hatherley.	Sir Roundell Palmer.
Earl Granville.	Mr. Henley.	Lord Lytton.
Lord Cairns.	The Duke of Argyll.	Late Earl of Derby.
Marquis of Hartington.	Sir Stafford Northcote.	Late Earl of Clarendon.
	Earl Grey.	

[*Just out.*

65, *Cornhill, and* 12, *Paternoster Row, London.*

XII.

BRIEFS AND PAPERS. Being Sketches of the Bar and the Press. By Two Idle Apprentices. Crown 8vo. 7s. 6d.

Our Leading Columns.
Our Special Correspondent.
Our Own Reporter.
In the Gallery.
Our Special Wire
The Story of the Fogborough Englishman.
In the Temple.

Westminster Hall.
On Circuit.
Scissors and Paste.
A Rising Junior.
Country Sessions.
An Eminent Leader.
Lincoln's Inn.
At the Old Bailey.

[*Just out.*

XIII.

SOLDIERING AND SCRIBBLING. By ARCHIBALD FORBES, of the *Daily News*, Author of "My Experience of the War between France and Germany." Crown 8vo. 7s. 6d.

A Penny a Day.
The Christmas Cattle Market.
Soldiers' Wives.
The Story of the Megæra.
In a Military Prison.
German War Prayers.
Flogged.
Sunday Afternoon at Guy's.
Butcher Jack's Story.

Bummarees.
A Deserter's Story.
Lions and Lion-Tamers.
Our March on Brighton.
Catsmeat.
Army Crimes and Punishments.
Whisky.
Furs.
Some Christmases.

[*Just out.*

XIV.

MEMOIRS OF MRS. LÆTITIA BOOTHBY. Written by herself in the year 1775. Edited by WILLIAM CLARK RUSSELL. Author of "The Book of Authors," etc. Crown 8vo. 7s. 6d.

XV.

MEMOIRS OF LEONORA CHRISTINA, Daughter of Christian IV. of Denmark. Written during her imprisonment in the Blue Tower of the Royal Palace at Copenhagen, 1663-1685. Translated by F. E. BUNNETT. With an Autotype Portrait of the Princess. Medium 8vo. 12s. 6d.

XVI.

THE FORMS OF WATER IN RAIN AND RIVERS, ICE AND GLACIERS. With 32 Illustrations. By J. TYNDALL, LL.D., F.R.S. *Being Vol. I. of The International Scientific Series.* Price 5s.

☞ Prospectuses of the Series may be had of the publishers. For full announcement of the Series, see the end of this Catalogue.

XVII.

CHANGE OF AIR AND SCENE. A Physician's Hints about Doctors, Patients, Hygiène, and Society; with Notes of Excursions for Health in the Pyrenees, and amongst the Watering-places of France (inland and seaward), Switzerland, Corsica, and the Mediterranean. By Dr. ALPHONSE DONNÉ. Large post 8vo. Price 9s.

Utility of Hygiène.	Hygiène of the Teeth.
The Hygiène of the Four Seasons.	Hygiène of the Stomach.
Exercise and Travels for Health.	Hygiène of the Eyes.
Mineral Waters.	Hygiène of Nervous Women.
Sea Baths.	The Toilet and Dress.
Hydro-Therapeutics.	Notes on Fever.

Hygiène of the Lungs.

"A useful and pleasantly-written book, containing many valuable hints on the general management of health from a shrewd and experienced medical man."—*Graphic*.

XVIII.
Second edition.

SEPTIMIUS. A Romance. By NATHANIEL HAWTHORNE, Author of "The Scarlet Letter," "Transformation," etc. One volume, crown 8vo. Cloth extra, gilt, 9s.

A peculiar interest attaches to this work. It was the last thing the author wrote, and he may be said to have died as he finished it.

The *Athenæum* says that "the book is full of Hawthorne's most characteristic writing."

"One of the best examples of Hawthorne's writing; every page is impressed with his peculiar view of thought, conveyed in his own familiar way."—*Post*.

XIX.

A TREATISE ON RELAPSING FEVER. By R. T. LYONS, Assistant-Surgeon Bengal Army. Small Post 8vo. 7s. 6d.

XX.

HEALTH AND DISEASE AS INFLUENCED BY THE DAILY, SEASONAL, AND OTHER CYCLICAL CHANGES IN THE HUMAN SYSTEM By Dr. EDWARD SMITH, F.R.S. A New Edition. 7s. 6d.

XXI.

CONSUMPTION IN ITS EARLY AND REMEDIABLE STAGES. By Dr. EDWARD SMITH, F.R.S. A New Edition. 7s. 6d.

65, *Cornhill, and* 12, *Paternoster Row, London.*

XXII.
PRACTICAL DIETARY FOR FAMILIES, SCHOOLS, AND THE LABOURING CLASSES. By Dr. EDWARD SMITH, F.R.S. A New Edition. Price 3*s*. 6*d*.

XXIII.
Second Edition.
HERMANN AGHA: An Eastern Narrative. By W. GIFFORD PALGRAVE, Author of "Travels in Central Arabia," etc. 2 vols., Crown 8vo. Cloth, extra gilt. 18*s*.

"Reads like a tale of life, with all its incidents. The young will take to it for its love portions, the older for its descriptions, some in this day for its Arab philosophy."—*Athenæum*.

"The cardinal merit, however, of the story is, to our thinking, the exquisite simplicity and purity of the love portion. There is a positive fragrance as of newly-mown hay about it, as compared with the artificially perfumed passions which are detailed to us with such gusto by our ordinary novel-writers in their endless volumes."—*Observer*.

XXIV.
NORMAN MACLEOD, D.D.: A Contribution towards his Biography. By ALEXANDER STRAHAN. 1*s*.

** Reprinted, with numerous Additions and many Illustrations from Sketches by Dr. Macleod, from the *Contemporary Review*.

XXV.
LIVES OF ENGLISH POPULAR LEADERS. No. 1. Stephen Langton. By C. EDMUND MAURICE. Crown 8vo. 7*s*. 6*d*.

"The volume contains many interesting details, including some important documents. It will amply repay those who read it, whether as a chapter of the constitutional history of England or as the life of a great Englishman."—*Spectator*.

"Mr. Maurice has written a very interesting book, which may be read with equal pleasure and profit."—*Morning Post*.

XXVI.
SIX PRIVY COUNCIL JUDGMENTS—1850–1872. Annotated by W. G. BROOKE, M.A., Barrister-at-Law. Cr. 8vo. 9*s*.

1. Gorham *v*. Bishop of Exeter.—2. Westerton *v*. Liddell.—3. Williams *v*. Bishop of Salisbury, and Wilson *v*. Fendal.—4. Martin *v*. Mackonochie. —5. Hibbert *v*. Purchas.—6. Sheppard *v*. Bennett.

65, Cornhill, and 12, Paternoster Row, London.

XXVII.

Second Edition.

THOUGHTS FOR THE TIMES. By the Rev. H. R. HAWEIS, M.A., Author of "Music and Morals," etc. Crown 8vo. 7s. 6d.

INTRODUCTORY.—I. The Liberal Clergy. GOD.—II. Conception III. Experience. CHRISTIANITY.—IV. Character. V. History. THE BIBLE.—VI. Essence. VII. Doctrine. THE ARTICLES.—VIII. The Trinity. ORIGINAL SIN. IX. Predestination. The Church. LIFE.—X. Pleasure. XI. Sacrifice. WORSHIP.—XII. The Lord's Day. XIII. Preaching. CONCLUSION.—XIV. The Law of Progress.

XXVIII.

Second Edition.

IN QUEST OF COOLIES. A South Sea Sketch. By JAMES L. A. HOPE. Crown 8vo, with 15 Illustrations from Sketches by the Author. Price 6s.

"Mr. Hope's description of the natives is graphic and amusing, and the book is altogether well worthy of perusal."—*Standard.*

"Lively and clever sketches."—*Athenæum.*

"This agreeably written and amusingly illustrated volume."—*Public Opinion.*

XXIX.

AN ESSAY ON THE CULTURE OF THE OBSERVING POWERS OF CHILDREN, especially in Connection with the Study of Botany. By ELIZA A. YOUMANS, of New York. Edited, with Notes and a Supplement on the Extension of the Principle to Elementary Intellectual Training in General, by JOSEPH PAYNE, Fellow of the College of Preceptors: Author of "Lectures on the Science and Art of Education," etc. Crown 8vo. 2s. 6d.

"The little book, now under notice, is expressly designed to make the earliest instruction of children a mental discipline. Miss Youmans presents in her work the ripe results of educational experience reduced to a system, wisely conceiving that an education—even the most elementary—should be regarded as a discipline of the mental powers, and that the facts of external nature supply the most suitable materials for this description in the case of children. She has applied that principle to the study of botany. This study, according to her just notions on the subject, is to be fundamentally based on the exercise of the pupil's own powers of observation. He is to see and examine the properties of plants and flowers at first hand, not merely to be informed of what others have seen and examined."—*Pall Mall Gazette.*

XXX.

From the Author's latest Stereotyped Edition.

MISS YOUMANS' FIRST BOOK OF BOTANY. Designed to cultivate the observing powers of children. New and Enlarged Edition, with 300 Engravings. Crown 8vo, 5s.

XXXI.

ALEXIS DE TOCQUEVILLE. Correspondence and Conversations with NASSAU W. SENIOR, from 1833 to 1859. Edited by Mrs. M. C. M. SIMPSON. Two Vols., Large Post 8vo, 21s.

"An extremely interesting book, and a singularly good illustration of the value which, even in an age of newspapers and magazines, memoirs have and will always continue to have for the purposes of history."—*Saturday Review.*

"A book replete with knowledge and thought."—*Quarterly Review.*

"Another of those interesting journals in which Mr. Senior has, as it were, crystallized the sayings of some of those many remarkable men with whom he came in contact."—*Morning Post.*

XXXII.

ECHOES OF A FAMOUS YEAR. By HARRIET PARR, Author of "The Life of Jeanne d'Arc," "In the Silver Age," etc. Crown 8vo, 8s. 6d.

"A graceful and touching, as well as truthful account of the Franco-Prussian War. Those who are in the habit of reading books to children will find this at once instructive and delightful."—*Public Opinion.*

"Miss Parr has the great gift of charming simplicity of style: and if children are not interested in her book, many of their seniors will be."—*British Quarterly Review.*

XXXIII.

ROUND THE WORLD IN 1870. A Volume of Travels, with Maps. By A. D. CARLISLE, B.A., Trin. Coll., Camb. Demy 8vo, 16s.

"Makes one understand how going round the world is to be done in the quickest and pleasantest manner, and how the brightest and most cheerful of travellers did it with eyes wide open and keen attention all on the alert, with ready sympathies, with the happiest facility of hitting upon the most interesting features of nature and the most interesting characteristics of man, and all for its own sake."—*Spectator.*

"We can only commend, which we do very heartily, an eminently sensible and readable book."—*British Quarterly Review.*

65, Cornhill, and 12, Paternoster Row, London.

XXXIV.

OVER VOLCANOES; OR, THROUGH FRANCE AND SPAIN IN 1871. By A. KINGSMAN. Crown 8vo. 10s. 6d.

"The writer's tone is so pleasant, his language is so good, and his spirits are so fresh, buoyant, and exhilarating, that you find yourself inveigled into reading, for the thousand-and-first time, a description of a Spanish bull-fight."—*Illustrated London News.*

"The adventures of our tourists are related with a good deal of pleasantry and humorous dash, which make the narrative agreeable reading." —*Public Opinion.*

"A work which we cordially recommend to such readers as desire to know something of Spain as she is to-day. Indeed, so fresh and original is it, that we could have wished that it had been a bigger book than it is." —*Literary World.*

XXXV.

Second Edition.

THE NILE WITHOUT A DRAGOMAN. By FREDERIC EDEN. In one vol., crown 8vo, cloth, 7s. 6d.

"Should any of our readers care to imitate Mr. Eden's example, and wish to see things with their own eyes, and shift for themselves, next winter in Upper Egypt, they will find this book a very agreeable guide."—*Times.*

"Gives, within moderate compass, a suggestive description of the charms, curiosities, dangers, and discomforts of the Nile voyage."—*Saturday Review.*

"We have in these pages the most minute description of life as it appeared on the banks of the Nile; all that could be seen or was worth seeing in nature or in art is here pleasantly and graphically set down. . . . It is a book to read during an autumn holiday."—*Spectator.*

XXXVI.

Second Edition.

THE SECRET OF LONG LIFE. Dedicated by special permission to LORD ST. LEONARDS. Large crown 8vo, 5s.

"A charming little volume, written with singular felicity of style and illustration."—*Times.*

"A very pleasant little book, which is always, whether it deal in paradox or earnest, cheerful, genial, scholarly."—*Spectator.*

"The bold and striking character of the whole conception is entitled to the warmest admiration."—*Pall Mall Gazette.*

"We should recommend our readers to get this book . . . because they will be amused by the jovial miscellaneous and cultured gossip with which he strews his pages."—*British Quarterly Review.*

65, *Cornhill, and* 12, *Paternoster Row, London.*

XXXVII.
Second Edition.
SCRIPTURE LANDS IN CONNECTION WITH THEIR HISTORY. By G. S. DREW, M.A., Vicar of Trinity, Lambeth, Author of "Reasons of Faith." Bevelled boards, 8vo, price 10s. 6d.

"Mr. Drew has invented a new method of illustrating Scripture history—from observation of the countries. Instead of narrating his travels and referring from time to time to the facts of sacred history belonging to the different countries, he writes an outline history of the Hebrew nation from Abraham downwards, with special reference to the various points in which the geography illustrates the history. The advantages of this plan are obvious. Mr. Drew thus gives us not a mere imitation of 'Sinai and Palestine,' but a view of the same subject from the other side. . . . He is very successful in picturing to his readers the scenes before his own mind. The position of Abraham in Palestine is portrayed, both socially and geographically, with great vigour. Mr. Drew has given an admirable account of the Hebrew sojourn in Egypt, and has done much to popularize the newly-acquired knowledge of Assyria in connection with the two Jewish kingdoms.—*Saturday Review.*

XXXVIII.
Second Edition.
CATHOLICISM AND THE VATICAN. With a Narrative of the Old Catholic Congresses at Munich and Cologne. By J. LOWRY WHITTLE, A.M., Trin. Coll., Dublin. Crown 8vo, 4s. 6d.

"We cannot follow the author through his graphic and lucid sketch of the Catholic movement in Germany and of the Munich Congress, at which he was present; but we may cordially recommend his book to all who wish to follow the course of the movement."—*Saturday Review.*

"A valuable and philosophic contribution to the solution of one of the greatest questions of this stirring age."—*Church Times.*

XXXIX.
NAZARETH: ITS LIFE AND LESSONS. In small 8vo, cloth, 5s. By the Author of "The Divine Kingdom on Earth as it is in Heaven."

"*In Him was life, and the life was the light of men.*"

"A singularly reverent and beautiful book; the style in which it is written is not less chaste and attractive than its subject."—*Daily Telegraph.*

"Perhaps one of the most remarkable books recently issued in the whole range of English theology. . . . Original in design, calm and appreciative in language, noble and elevated in style, this book, we venture to think, will live."—*Churchman's Magazine.*

65, *Cornhill, and* 12, *Paternoster Row, London.*

XL.

JOURNALS KEPT IN FRANCE AND ITALY, FROM 1848 TO 1852. With a Sketch of the Revolution of 1848. By the late NASSAU WILLIAM SENIOR. Edited by his daughter, M. C. M. SIMPSON. In two vols., post 8vo, 24s.

"The present volume gives us conversations with some of the most prominent men in the political history of France and Italy . . . as well as with others whose names are not so familiar or are hidden under initials. Mr. Senior has the art of inspiring all men with frankness, and of persuading them to put themselves unreservedly in his hands without ear of private circulation."—*Athenæum.*

"The book has a genuine historical value."—*Saturday Review.*

"No better, more honest, and more readable view of the state of political society during the existence of the second Republic could well be looked for."—*Examiner.*

XLI.

THE DIVINE KINGDOM ON EARTH AS IT IS IN HEAVEN. In demy 8vo, bound in cloth. Price 10s. 6d. "Our COMMONWEALTH is in Heaven." [*Now ready.*

"It is seldom that, in the course of our critical duties, we have to deal with a volume of any size or pretension so entirely valuable and satisfactory as this. Published anonymously as it is, there is no living divine to whom the authorship would not be a credit. . . . Not the least of its merits is the perfect simplicity and clearness, conjoined with a certain massive beauty, of its style."—*Literary Churchman.*

"A high purpose and a devout spirit characterize this work. It is thoughtful and eloquent. . . . The most valuable and suggestive chapter is entitled 'Fulfilment in Life and Ministry of Christ,' which is full of original thinking admirably expressed."—*British Quarterly Review.*

65, *Cornhill, and* 12, *Paternoster Row, London.*

FORTHCOMING NOVELS.

I.

A LITTLE WORLD. By GEO. MANVILLE FENN, Author of "The Sapphire Cross," "Mad," etc. Three vols.

II.

CIVIL SERVICE. By J. T. LISTADO, Author of "Maurice Reynhart." 2 vols.

III.

VANESSA. By the Author of "Thomasina," &c. 2 vols.

IV.

THE QUEEN'S SHILLING. By Capt. ARTHUR GRIFFITHS, Author of "Peccavi; or, Geoffrey Singleton's Mistake." 2 vols.

V.

CHESTERLEIGH. By ANSLEY CONYERS. 3 vols.

VI.

SQUIRE SILCHESTER'S WHIM. By MORTIMER COLLINS, Author of "Marquis and Merchant," "The Princess Clarice," &c. 3 vols.

VII.

WHAT 'TIS TO LOVE. By the Author of "Flora Adair," "The Value of Fosterstown," etc. Three vols.

VIII.

JOHANNES OLAF. By E. DE WILLE. Translated by F. E. BUNNETT.

The author of this story enjoys a high reputation in Germany; and both English and German critics have spoken in terms of the warmest praise of this and her previous stories. She has been called "The 'George Eliot' of Germany."

IX.

TOO LATE. By Mrs. NEWMAN. Two vols., crown 8vo.

X.

LISETTE'S VENTURE. By Mrs. RUSSELL GRAY. Two vols., crown 8vo.

65, Cornhill, and 12, Paternoster Row, London.

Recently Published Novels.

I.
SEETA. By Col. MEADOWS TAYLOR, Author of "Tara," etc. In three vols. [*Just out.*

II.
THE DOCTOR'S DILEMMA. By HESBA STRETTON, Author of "Little Meg," etc., etc.
[*Just out.*

III.
OFF THE SKELLIGS. By JEAN INGELOW. (Her first Romance.) In four vols.
[*Just out.*

IV.
HONOR BLAKE; THE STORY OF A PLAIN WOMAN. By Mrs. KEATINGE, Author of "English Homes in India." Two vols., crown 8vo. [*Just out.*

V.
THE SPINSTERS OF BLATCHINGTON. By MAR. TRAVERS. Two vols., crown 8vo.

"A pretty story. In all respects deserving of a favourable reception."—*Graphic.*
"A book of more than average merit, and worth reading."—*Examiner.*

VI.
THE PRINCESS CLARICE. A STORY OF 1871. By MORTIMER COLLINS. Two vols., crown 8vo.

"Mr. Collins has produced a readable book, amusingly characteristic. There is good description of Devonshire scenery; and lastly there is Clarice, a most successful heroine, who must speak to the reader for herself."—*Athenæum.*
"Very readable and amusing. We would especially give an honourable mention to Mr. Collins' '*vers de société*,' the writing of which has almost become a lost art."—*Pall Mall Gazette.*
"A bright, fresh, and original book, with which we recommend all genuine novel-readers to become acquainted at the earliest opportunity."—*Standard.*

VII.
A GOOD MATCH. By AMELIA PERRIER. Author of "Mea Culpa." Two vols. [*Just out.*

"Racy and lively."—*Athenæum.*
"Agreeably written."—*Public Opinion.*
"As pleasant and readable a novel as we have seen this season."—*Examiner.*
"This clever and amusing novel."—*Pall Mall Gazette.*

VIII.
THOMASINA. By the Author of "Dorothy," "De Cressy," etc. Two vols., crown 8vo.
[*Just out.*

"We would liken it to a finished and delicate cabinet picture, in which there is no brilliant colour, and yet all is harmony; in which no line is without its purpose, but all contribute to the unity of the work."—*Athenæum.*
"For the delicacies of character-drawing, for play of incident, and for finish o style, we must refer our readers to the story itself: from the perusal of which they cannot fail to derive both interest and amusement."—*Daily News.*
"This undeniably pleasing story."—*Pall Mall Gazette.*

IX.
CRUEL AS THE GRAVE. By the COUNTESS VON BOTHMER. Three vols., crown 8vo.

"*Jealousy is cruel as the Grave.*"

"The Wise Man's motto is prefixed to an interesting, though somewhat tragic story, by the Countess von Bothmer.... Her German prince, with his chivalrous affection, his disinterested patriotism, and his soldierlike sense of duty, is no unworthy type of a national character which has lately given the world many instances of old-fashioned heroism."—*Athenæum.*
"An agreeable, unaffected, and eminently readable novel."—*Daily News.*

65, *Cornhill, and* 12, *Paternoster Row, London.*

X.
THE STORY OF SIR EDWARD'S WIFE. By HAMILTON MARSHALL, Author of "For Very Life." One vol., crown 8vo. [*Just out.*

"There are many clever conceits in it. ... Mr. Hamilton Marshall proves in 'Sir Edward's Wife' that he can tell a story closely and pleasantly."—*Pall Mall Gazette.*

"A quiet graceful little story."—*Spectator.*

XI.
PERPLEXITY. By SYDNEY MOSTYN. Three vols., cr. 8vo.

"Shows much lucidity, much power of portraiture, and no inconsiderable sense of humour."—*Examiner.*

"The literary workmanship is good, and the story forcibly and graphically told."—*Daily News.*

"Written with very considerable power; the plot is original and ... worked out with great cleverness and sustained interest."—*Standard.*

XII.
LINKED AT LAST. By F. E. BUNNETT. One vol., cr. 8vo.

"'Linked at Last' contains so much of pretty description, natural incident, and delicate portraiture, that the reader who once takes it up will not be inclined to relinquish it without concluding the volume." *Morning Post.*

"A very charming story."—*John Bull.*

XIII.
HER TITLE OF HONOUR. By HOLME LEE. One vol., crown 8vo. (Second Edition.)

"It is unnecessary to recommend tales of Holme Lee's, for they are well known, and all more or less liked. But this book far exceeds even our favourites, *Sylvan Holt's Daughter, Kathie Brande,* and *Thorney Hall,* because with the interest of a pathetic story is united the value of a definite and high purpose."—*Spectator.*

"A most exquisitely written story."—*Literary Churchman.*

BOOKS FOR THE YOUNG.

I.
BRAVE MEN'S FOOTSTEPS. A Book of Example and Anecdote for Young People. By the EDITOR of "Men who have Risen." With four Illustrations by C. DOYLE. Crown 8vo. 3*s.* 6*d.*

Josiah Wedgwood — the Man of Energy.
Granville Sharp — the Negro's earliest Friend.
Richard Cobden—the International Man.
Dr. William Smith—the Father of English Geology.
Andrew Reed — the Stay of the Hopeless.

Michael Faraday — the Refined Philosopher.
Thomas Wright—the Prison Philanthropist.
Joseph Paxton—the Gardener Architect.
The Early Life of the late Prince Consort.
Etc., etc.

65, Cornhill, and 12, Paternoster Row, London.

II.

Just ready, gilt cloth and gilt edges, price 7s. 6d., the Volume for 1872, of

GOOD WORDS FOR THE YOUNG. Containing Numerous Contributions by

NORMAN MACLEOD, D.D.	A. L. WARING.
THE AUTHOR OF "PATTY."	W. ALLINGHAM.
LADY BARKER.	MRS. GEORGE CUPPLES.
JEAN INGELOW.	ROBERT BUCHANAN.
C. C. FRASER-TYTLER.	

And about One Hundred and Fifty Illustrations by

ARTHUR HUGHES.	W. J. WIEGAND.	F. S. WALKER.
J. MAHONEY.	TOWNLEY GREEN.	M. FRASER-TYTLER.
J. B. ZWECKER.	F. A. FRASER.	

III.

THE LITTLE WONDER-HORN. By JEAN INGELOW. A Second Series of "Stories told to a Child." 15 Illustrations. Cloth gilt, 3s. 6d.

IV.

GUTTA-PERCHA WILLIE: THE WORKING GENIUS. By GEORGE MACDONALD. With Illustrations by ARTHUR HUGHES. Crown 8vo, 3s. 6d.

V.

PLUCKY FELLOWS. A Book for Boys. By STEPHEN J. MACKENNA. Illustrated.

VI.

HOITY TOITY, THE GOOD LITTLE FELLOW. By CHARLES CAMDEN, Author of "The Boys of Axleford." Illustrated. Crown 8vo, 3s. 6d.

VII.

STORIES IN PRECIOUS STONES. By HELEN ZIMMERN. Crown 8vo. Six Illustrations. Price 5s.

65, Cornhill, and 12, Paternoster Row, London.

VIII.
THE TRAVELLING MENAGERIE. By CHARLES CAMDEN, Author of "Hoity Toity." Illustrated by J. MAHONEY. Crown 8vo, 3s. 6d.

IX.
THE DESERTED SHIP. A Real Story of the Atlantic. By CUPPLES HOWE, Master Mariner. Illustrated by TOWNLEY GREEN. Crown 8vo, 3s. 6d.

X.
ELSIE DINSMORE. By MARTHA FARQUHARSON. Crown 8vo. Illustrated.

XI.
HOLIDAYS AT ROSELANDS. With some after scenes in Elsie's life. Being a Sequel to "Elsie Dinsmore." By MARTHA FARQUHARSON. Crown 8vo. Illustrated.

XII.
ELSIE'S GIRLHOOD. A Sequel to "Elsie Dinsmore" and "Elsie's Holidays at Roselands." By MARTHA FARQUHARSON.

XIII.
JEAN JAROUSSEAU, THE PASTOR OF THE DESERT. From the French of EUGÈNE PELLETAN. Translated by Colonel E. P. DE L'HOSTE. In fcap. 8vo, with an engraved frontispiece, price 5s.

"There is a poetical simplicity and picturesqueness; the noblest heroism; unpretentious religion; pure love, and the spectacle of a household brought up in the fear of the Lord. . . . The whole story has an air of quaint antiquity similar to that which invests with a charm more easily felt than described the site of some splendid ruin."—*Illustrated London News.*

"A touching record of the struggles in the cause of religious liberty of a real man."—*Graphic.*

XIV.
LILLIPUT REVELS. By the Author of "Lilliput Levée." With Illustrations. Crown 8vo, 3s. 6d. [*Shortly.*

MILITARY WORKS.

I.
ARMY RESERVES AND MILITIA REFORMS. By Lieut.-Col. The Hon. C. ANSON.
[*In the press.*

II.
VICTORIES AND DEFEATS. An attempt to explain the causes which have led to them. An Officer's Manual. By Col. R. P. ANDERSON. Demy 8vo.
[*In preparation.*

III.
Shortly will be published:
STUDIES IN THE NEW INFANTRY TACTICS. By Major W. von SCHEREFF. Translated from the German.

IV.
THE OPERATIONS OF THE FIRST ARMY TO THE CAPITULATION OF METZ. By VON SCHELL, Major in the Chief General Staff, with Maps, including one of Metz and of the country around, which will be the most perfect yet published of that district. In demy 8vo. Uniform with the above.
[*In preparation.*

*** The most important events described in this work are the battles of Spichern, those before Metz on the 14th and 18th August, and (on this point nothing authentic has yet been published) the history of the investment of Metz (battle of Noisseville).

This work, however, possesses a greater importance than that derived from these points, because it represents for the first time from the official documents the generalship of Von Steinmetz. Hitherto we have had no exact reports on the deeds and motives of this celebrated general. This work has the special object of unfolding carefully the relations in which the commander of the First Army acted, the plan of operations which he drew up, and the manner in which he carried it out.

V.
THE OPERATIONS OF THE GERMAN ARMIES IN FRANCE, FROM SEDAN TO THE END OF THE WAR OF 1870-1. With large Official Map. From the Journals of the Head-Quarters Staff. By Major WM. BLUME, of the Prussian Ministry of War. Translated by E. M. JONES, Major 20th Foot, late Professor of Military History, Sandhurst. Demy 8vo. Price 9s.

"The work of Major von Blume in its English dress forms the most valuable addition to our stock of works upon the war that our press has put forth. Major Blume writes with a clear conciseness much wanting in many of his country's historians, and Major Jones has done himself and his original alike justice by his vigorous yet correct translation of the excellent volume on which he has laboured. Our space forbids our doing more than commending it earnestly as the most authentic and instructive narrative of the second section of the war that has yet appeared."—*Saturday Review.*

"The book is of absolute necessity to the military student. : . . The work is one of high merit and . . . has the advantage of being rendered into fluent English, and is accompanied by an excellent military map."—*United Service Gazette.*

"The work of translation has been well done; the expressive German idioms have been rendered into clear nervous English without losing any of their original force; and in notes, prefaces, and introductions, much additional information has been given."—*Athenæum.*

65, *Cornhill, and* 12, *Paternoster Row, London.*

VI.
THE OPERATIONS OF THE SOUTH ARMY IN JANUARY AND FEBRUARY, 1871. Compiled from the Official War Documents of the Head-Quarters of the Southern Army. By Count HERMANN VON WARTENSLEBEN, Colonel in the Prussian General Staff. Translated by Colonel C. H. VON WRIGHT. Demy 8vo., with Maps. Uniform with the above. Price 6s.

VII.
THE CAMPAIGN OF THE FIRST ARMY IN NORTHERN FRANCE. (Against Faidherbe.) By Colonel Count HERMANN VON WARTENSLEBEN, Chief of the Staff of the First Army. In demy 8vo. Uniform with the above. [*In preparation.*

N.B.—It is believed that General BEAUCHAMP WALKER, of Berlin, will translate this work.

VIII.
TACTICAL DEDUCTIONS FROM THE WAR OF 1870-1. By Captain A. VON BOGUSLAWSKI. Translated by Colonel LUMLEY GRAHAM, Late 18th (Royal Irish) Regiment. Demy 8vo. Uniform with the above. Price 7s.

"In all essential things, according to our conviction, the author has rightly apprehended the lessons of the late war, and his views are a guide and criterion that will be of service to every officer."—*Militair Wochenblatt.*

"Major Boguslawski's tactical deductions from the war are, that infantry still preserve their superiority over cavalry, that open order must henceforth be the main principles of all drill, and that the chassepot is the best of all small arms for precision. . . . We must, without delay, impress brain and forethought into the British Service; and we cannot commence the good work too soon, or better, than by placing the two books ('The Operations of the German Armies' and 'Tactical Deductions') we have here criticised, in every military library, and introducing them as class-books in every tactical school."—*United Service Gazette.*

IX.
HASTY INTRENCHMENTS. By A. BRIALMONT, Colonel on the Belgian Staff. Translated by CHARLES A. EMPSON, Lieutenant R.A. Nine Plates. Price 6s.

X.
CAVALRY FIELD DUTY. By Major-General VON MIRUS. Translated by Capt. FRANK S. RUSSELL, 14th (King's) Hussars. Crown 8vo, limp cloth, 5s.

*** This is the text-book of instruction in the German cavalry, and comprises all the details connected with the military duties of cavalry soldiers on service. The translation is made from a new edition, which contains the modifications introduced consequent on the experiences of the late war. The great interest that students feel in all the German military methods, will it is believed, render this book especially acceptable at the present time.

XI.
THE ARMY OF THE NORTH-GERMAN CONFEDERATION. A brief description of its organization, of the different branches of the Service and their *rôle* in war, of its mode of fighting," etc. By a PRUSSIAN GENERAL. Translated from the German by Col. EDWARD NEWDIGATE. Demy 8vo. 5s.

*** The authorship of this book was erroneously ascribed to the renowned General von Moltke, but there can be little doubt that it was written under his immediate inspiration.

65, Cornhill, and 12, Paternoster Row, London.

XII.

Now ready, an authorised and accurate Translation of

STUDIES IN LEADING TROOPS. By Col. VON VERDU DU VERNOIS. Translated by Lieut. H. J. T. HILLYARD, 71st Foot. Parts I. and II. Demy 8vo, price 7s.

Notice.—The German publishers of this work desire to make it known that the author protests against an edition of Part I. which is on sale in England, and which is both an inaccurate and unauthorised translation.

⁎⁎* General BEAUCHAMP WALKER says of this work:—" I recommend the first two numbers of Colonel von Verdy's 'Studies' to the attentive perusal of my brother officers. They supply a want which I have often felt during my service in this country, namely, a minuter tactical detail of the minor operations of the war than any but the most observant and fortunately placed staff officer is in a position to give. I have read and re-read them very carefully, I hope with profit, certainly with great interest, and believe that practice, in the sense of these 'Studies,' would be a valuable preparation for manœuvres on a more extended scale."—Berlin, June, 1872.

XIII.

DISCIPLINE AND DRILL. Four Lectures delivered to the London Scottish Rifle Volunteers. By Captain S. FLOOD PAGE, Adjutant of the Regiment, late 105th Light Infantry, and Adjutant of the Edinburgh Rifle Brigade. Just published. A Cheaper Edition, price 1s.

"One of the best-known and coolest-headed of the metropolitan regiments, whose adjutant moreover has lately published an admirable collection of lectures addressed by him to the men of his corps."—*Times.*

"The very useful and interesting work. . . . Every Volunteer, officer or private, will be the better for perusing and digesting the plain-spoken truths which Captain Page so firmly, and yet so modestly, puts before them; and we trust that the little book in which they are contained will find its way into all parts of Great Britain."—*Volunteer Service Gazette.*

XIV.
AUTHORISED TRANSLATION.

THE FRANCO-GERMAN WAR, 1870-71. First Part:— History of the War to the Downfall of the Empire. First Section:— The events in July. Translated from the German Official Account at the Topographical and Statistical Department of the War Office. By Capt. F. C. H. CLARKE, R.A. First Section, with Map, now Ready. Demy 8vo, 3s.

XV.

THE SUBSTANTIVE SENIORITY ARMY LIST. Majors and Captains. Containing the Names of all Substantive Majors and Captains, Serving upon Full-pay or Retired upon Half-pay, arranged according to their Seniority in the Service, and in such order as immediately to exhibit the standing of every such Major or Captain for Promotion in his own arm of the Service, whether Cavalry, Artillery, Engineers, Infantry, or Marines, specifying their particular Corps, and distinguishing those holding Higher Brevet-rank. By Capt. F. B. P. WHITE, 1st W. I. Regiment. 8vo, sewed, 2s. 6d.

THE BENGAL QUARTERLY	ARMY LIST.		Sewed, 15s.
THE BOMBAY	DO.	DO.	Sewed, 9s.
THE MADRAS	DO.	DO.	Sewed, 12s.

65, *Cornhill, and* 12, *Paternoster Row, London.*

The Cornhill Library of Fiction.

It is intended in this Series to produce books of such merit that readers will care to preserve them on their shelves. They are well printed on good paper, handsomely bound, with a Frontispiece, and are sold at the moderate price of

3s. 6d. each.

I.
ROBIN GRAY. By CHARLES GIBBON. With a Frontispiece by HENNESSY. [*Ready*.

II.
KITTY. By Miss M. BETHAM-EDWARDS. [*Ready*.

III.
HIRELL. By JOHN SAUNDERS, Author of "Abel Drake's Wife." [*Ready*.

IV.
ONE OF TWO. By J. HAIN FRISWELL, Author of "The Gentle Life," etc.

V.
READY MONEY MORTIBOY. [*At Christmas*.

Other Standard Novels to follow.

Poetry.

I.
CALDERON.—THE PURGATORY OF ST. PATRICK—THE WONDERFUL MAGICIAN — LIFE IS A DREAM. Translated from the Spanish of Calderon, by DENIS FLORENCE MACARTHY.

II.
SONGS FOR SAILORS. By W. C. BENNETT. Crown 8vo, 3s. 6d. With Steel Portrait and Illustrations.

An Edition in Illustrated paper Covers, price 1s.

65, Cornhill, and 12, Paternoster Row, London.

III.

Shortly will be Re-issued, with additions to each part, W. C. BENNETT'S POEMS, *in Five Parts, at One Shilling each.*

BABY MAY, THE WORN WEDDING RING, AND OTHER HOME POEMS. With Illustrations by WATSON.

QUEEN ELEANOR'S VENGEANCE, BALLADS, AND NARRATIVE POEMS. With Illustrations by WATSON.

SONGS BY A SONG-WRITER. With Steel Portrait. First Series.

SONGS BY A SONG-WRITER. With Illustrations by WATSON. Second Series.

POEMS OF THOUGHT AND FANCY, AND ONE HUNDRED SONNETS. With Illustrations by WATSON.

IV.

PREPARING FOR PUBLICATION.

A Collected Edition, in Five Volumes of

THE POETICAL AND PROSE WORKS OF ROBERT BUCHANAN.

V.

WALLED IN, AND OTHER POEMS. By the Rev. HENRY J. BULKELY. Crown 8vo, 5s.
[*Now Ready.*

VI.

SONGS OF LIFE AND DEATH. By JOHN PAYNE, Author of "Intaglios," "Sonnets," "The Masque of Shadows," etc. Cr. 8vo, 5s. [*Just out.*

VII.

SONGS OF TWO WORLDS. By a NEW WRITER. Fcap. 8vo, cloth, 5s.

"The 'New Writer' is certainly no tyro. No one after reading the first two poems, almost perfect in rhythm and all the graceful reserve of true lyrical strength, can doubt that this book is the result of lengthened thought and assiduous training in poetical form. . . . These poems will assuredly take high rank among the class to which they belong."—*British Quarterly Review, April 1st.*

"No extracts could do justice to the exquisite tones, the felicitous phrasing and delicately wrought harmonies of some of these poems."—*Nonconformist, March 27th.*

"Are we in this book making the acquaintance of a fine and original poet, or of a most artistic imitator? And our deliberate opinion is that the former hypothesis is the right one. It has a purity and delicacy of feeling like morning air."—*Graphic, March 16th.*

"If these poems are the mere preludes of a mind growing in power and in inclination for verse, we have in them the promise of a fine poet. . . . The verse describing Socrates has the highest note of critical poetry."—*Spectator, Feb. 17th.*

VIII.

EROS AGONISTES. By E. B. D. Crown 8vo, 3s. 6d.

"The author of these verses has written a very touching story of the human heart in the story he tells with such pathos and power, of an affection cherished so long and so secretly. . . . It is not the least merit of these pages that they are everywhere illumined with moral and religious sentiment suggested, not paraded, of the brightest, purest character."—*Standard.*

65, Cornhill, and 12, Paternoster Row, London.

IX.
THE LEGENDS OF ST. PATRICK, & OTHER POEMS.
By AUBREY DE VERE. Crown 8vo, 5s.

"We have marked, in almost every page, excellent touches from which we know not how to select. We have but space to commend the varied structure of his verse, the carefulness of his grammar, and his excellent English. All who believe that poetry should raise and not debase the social ideal, all who think that wit should exalt our standard of thought and manners, must welcome this contribution at once to our knowledge of the past and to the science of noble life.—*Saturday Review.*

X.
THE INN OF STRANGE MEETINGS, AND OTHER POEMS. By MORTIMER COLLINS. Crown 8vo, 5s.

"Mr. Collins has an undercurrent of chivalry and romance beneath the trifling vein of good humoured banter which is the special characteristic of his verse. . . . The 'Inn of Strange Meetings' s a sprightly piece."—*Athenæum.*

"Abounding in quiet humour, in bright fancy, in sweetness and melody of expression, and, at times, in the tenderest ouches of pathos."—*Graphic.*

XI.
ASPROMONTE, AND OTHER POEMS. Second Edition, cloth, 4s. 6d.

"The volume is anonymous; but there is no reason for the author to be ashamed of it. The 'Poems of Italy' are evidently inspired by genuine enthusiasm in the cause espoused; and one of them, 'The Execution of Felice Orsini,' has much poetic merit, the event celebrated being told with dramatic force."—*Athenæum.*

"The verse is fluent and free."—*Spectator.*

XII.
THE DREAM AND THE DEED, AND OTHER POEMS.
By PATRICK SCOTT, Author of "Footpaths Between Two Worlds," etc. Fcap. 8vo, cloth, 5s.

"A bitter and able satire on the vice and follies of the day, literary, social, and political."—*Standard.*

"Shows real poetic power coupled with evidences of satirical energy."—*Edinburgh Daily Review.*

●

65, Cornhill, and 12, Paternoster Row, London.

LIFE AND WORKS OF THE REV. FRED. W. ROBERTSON.

NEW AND CHEAPER EDITIONS.

LIFE AND LETTERS OF THE LATE REV. FRED. W. ROBERTSON, M.A. Edited by STOPFORD BROOKE, M.A., Hon. Chaplain in Ordinary to the Queen. Library Edition, in demy 8vo, with Steel Portrait. 12s.

A Popular Edition, in one vol., price 6s., is now ready.

A New Edition, in two volumes, uniform with the Sermons, price 7s. 6d., will be ready shortly.

SERMONS :—Price 3s. 6d. per vol.

First Series.	.	.	.	.	Small crown 8vo.
Second Series	.	.	.	.	Small crown 8vo.
Third Series	.	.	.	.	Small crown 8vo.
Fourth Series	.	.	.	.	Small crown 8vo.

EXPOSITORY LECTURES ON ST. PAUL'S EPISTLE TO THE CORINTHIANS. Small crown 8vo. 5s.

AN ANALYSIS OF MR. TENNYSON'S "IN MEMORIAM." (Dedicated by permission to the Poet-Laureate.) Fcap. 8vo. 2s.

THE EDUCATION OF THE HUMAN RACE. Translated from the German of GOTTHOLD EPHRAIM LESSING. Fcap. 8vo. 2s. 6d.

IN PREPARATION.

LECTURES AND ADDRESSES ON LITERARY AND SOCIAL TOPICS. Small crown 8vo. 3s. 6d.

A LECTURE ON FRED. W. ROBERTSON, M.A. By the Rev. F. A. NOBLE, delivered before the Young Men's Christian Association of Pittsburgh, U.S. 1s. 6d.

65, Cornhill, and 12, Paternoster Row, London.

SERMONS BY THE REV. STOPFORD A. BROOKE, M.A.
Honorary Chaplain to Her Majesty the Queen.

I.

THE LIFE AND WORK OF FREDERICK DENISON MAURICE. A Memorial Sermon. Crown 8vo, sewed. 1s.

II.

CHRIST IN MODERN LIFE. Sermons preached in St. James's Chapel, York Street, London. Third Edition. Crown 8vo. 7s. 6d.

"Nobly fearless and singularly strong . . . carries our admiration throughout."—*British Quarterly Review.*

III.

FREEDOM IN THE CHURCH OF ENGLAND. Second Edition. Six Sermons suggested by the Voysey Judgment. In One Volume. Crown 8vo, cloth, 3s. 6d.

"Every one should read them. No one can be insensible to the charm of his style, or the clear logical manner in which he treats his subject."—*Churchman's Monthly.*

"We have to thank Mr. Brooke for a very clear and courageous exposition of theological views, with which we are for the most part in full sympathy."—*Spectator.*

"Interesting and readable, and characterized by great clearness of thought, frankness of statement, and moderation of tone."—*Church Opinion.*

"A very fair statement of the views in respect to freedom of thought held by the liberal party in the Church of England."—*Blackwood's Magazine.*

IV.

SERMONS PREACHED IN ST. JAMES'S CHAPEL, YORK STREET, LONDON. Sixth Edition. Crown 8vo. 6s.

"No one who reads these sermons will wonder that Mr. Brooke is a great power in London, that his chapel is thronged, and his followers large and enthusiastic. They are fiery, energetic, impetuous sermons, rich with the treasures of a cultivated imagination."—*Guardian.*

"Mr. Brooke's sermons are shrewd and clever, and always readable. He is better off than many preachers, for he has something to say, and says it."—*Churchman's Magazine.*

"A fine specimen of the best preaching of the Episcopal pulpit."—*British Quarterly.*

65, Cornhill, and 12, Paternoster Row, London.

Books on Indian Subjects.

I.

THE EUROPEAN IN INDIA. A Hand-book of practical information for those proceeding to, or residing in, the East Indies, relating to Outfits, Routes, Time for Departure, Indian Climate, etc. By EDMUND C. P. HULL. With a MEDICAL GUIDE FOR ANGLO-INDIANS. Being a compendium of Advice to Europeans in India, relating to the Preservation and Regulation of Health. By R. S. MAIR, M.D., F.R.C.S.E., late Deputy Coroner of Madras. In one vol., Post 8vo, 6s.

"Full of all sorts of useful information to the English settler or traveller in India."—*Standard.*

"One of the most valuable books ever published in India—valuable for its sound information, its careful array of pertinent facts, and its sterling common sense. It is a publisher's as well as an author's 'hit,' for it supplies a want which few persons may have discovered, but which everybody will at once recognise when once the contents of the book have been mastered. The medical part of the work is invaluable."—*Calcutta Guardian.*

II.

EASTERN EXPERIENCES. By L. BOWRING, C.S.I., Lord Canning's Private Secretary, and for many years the Chief Commissioner of Mysore and Coorg. In one vol., demy 8vo, 16s. Illustrated with Maps and Diagrams.

"An admirable and exhaustive geographical, political, and industrial survey."—*Athenæum.*

"The usefulness of this compact and methodical summary of the most authentic information relating to countries whose welfare is intimately connected with our own, should obtain for Mr. Lewin Bowring's work a good place among treatises of its kind."—*Daily News.*

"Interesting even to the general reader, but more especially so to those who may have a special concern in that portion of our Indian Empire."—*Post.*

"An elaborately got up and carefully compiled work."—*Home News.*

III.

A MEMOIR OF THE INDIAN SURVEYS. By CLEMENT R. MARKHAM. Printed by order of Her Majesty's Secretary of State for India in Council. Imperial 8vo, 10s. 6d.

IV.

WESTERN INDIA BEFORE AND DURING THE MUTINIES. Pictures drawn from Life. By Major-General Sir GEORGE LE GRAND JACOB, K.C.S.I., C.B. In one vol., crown 8vo, 7s. 6d.

"The most important contribution to the history of Western India during the Mutinies, which has yet, in a popular form, been made public."—*Athenæum.*

"The legacy of a wise veteran, intent on the benefit of his countrymen rather than on the acquisition of fame."—*London and China Express.*

"Few men more competent than himself to speak authoritatively concerning Indian affairs."—*Standard.*

65, *Cornhill, and* 12, *Paternoster Row, London.*

V.

EXCHANGE TABLES OF STERLING AND INDIAN RUPEE CURRENCY, upon a new and extended system, embracing values from one farthing to one hundred thousand pounds, and at rates progressing, in sixteenths of a penny, from 1s. 9d. to 2s. 3d. per rupee. By DONALD FRASER, Accountant to the British Indian Steam Navigation Co., Limited. Royal 8vo, 10s. 6d.

VI.

A CATALOGUE OF MAPS OF THE BRITISH POSSESSIONS IN INDIA AND OTHER PARTS OF ASIA. Published by Order of Her Majesty's Secretary of State for India in Council. Royal 8vo, sewed, 1s.

A continuation of the above, sewed, price 6d., is now ready.

☞ *Messrs. Henry S. King & Co. are the authorised agents by the Government for the sale of the whole of the Maps enumerated in this Catalogue.*

Now Ready, crown 8vo, price 5s.

THE FORMS OF WATER IN RAIN AND RIVERS, ICE AND GLACIERS. With 32 Illustrations. By J. TYNDALL, LL.D., F.R.S.

Just Out, crown 8vo, price 4s.

PHYSICS AND POLITICS; or, Thoughts on the Application of the Principles of Natural Selection and Inheritance to Political Society. By WALTER BAGEHOT.

BEING VOLUMES ONE AND TWO OF

THE

INTERNATIONAL SCIENTIFIC SERIES.

MESSRS. HENRY S. KING & CO. have the pleasure to announce that under this title they are issuing a SERIES of POPULAR TREATISES, embodying the results of the latest investigations in the various departments of Science at present most prominently before the world.

The character and scope of the Series will be best indicated by a reference to the names and subjects included in the following List; from which it will be seen that the co-operation of many of the most distinguished Professors in England, America, Germany, and France has been already secured.

Although these Works are not specially designed for the instruction of beginners, still, as they are intended to address the *non-scientific public*, they will be, as far as possible, explanatory in character, and free from technicalities. The object of each author will be to bring his subject as near as he can to the general reader.

The Series will also be published simultaneously in New York by Messrs. D. Appleton & Co.; in Paris by M. Germer Baillière; and in Leipzig by Messrs. Brockhaus. The volumes will all be crown 8vo size, well printed on good paper, strongly and elegantly bound, and will sell in this country at a price *not exceeding Five Shillings*.

The next volume will be

FOOD. By Dr. EDWARD SMITH, F.R.S.

☞ Prospectuses of the Series may be had of the Publishers.

INTERNATIONAL SCIENTIFIC SERIES—FIRST LIST.

Prof. T. H. Huxley, LL.D., F.R.S.
Bodily Motion and Consciousness.

Dr. W. B. Carpenter, LL.D., F.R.S.
The Principles of Mental Physiology.

Sir John Lubbock, Bart., F.R.S.
The Antiquity of Man.

Prof. Rudolph Virchow.
Morbid Physiological Action.

Prof. Alexander Bain, LL.D.
Relations of Mind and Body.

Prof. Balfour Stewart, LL.D., F.R.S.
The Conservation of Energy.

Walter Bagehot, Esq.
Physics and Politics.

Dr. H. Charlton Bastian, M.D., F.R.S.
The Brain as an Organ of Mind.

Herbert Spencer, Esq.
The Study of Sociology.

Prof. William Odling, F.R.S.
The New Chemistry.

Prof. W. Thiselton Dyer, B.A., B.Sc.
Form and Habit in Flowering Plants.

Dr. Edward Smith, F.R.S.
Food.

Prof. W. Kingdom Clifford, M.A.
The First Principles of the Exact Sciences explained to the non-mathematical.

Mr. J. N. Lockyer, F.R.S.
Spectrum Analysis.

W. Lauder Lindsay, M.D., F.R.S.E.
Mind in the Lower Animals.

Dr. J. B. Pettigrew, M.D., F.R.S.
Walking, Swimming, and Flying.

Prof. John Tyndall, LL.D., F.R.S.
The Forms of Water in Rain and Rivers, Ice and Glaciers.

Prof. A. C. Ramsay, LL.D., F.R.S.
Earth Sculpture: Hills, Valleys, Mountains, Plains, Rivers, Lakes; how they were Produced, and how they have been Destroyed.

Dr. Henry Maudsley.
Responsibility in Disease.

Prof. W. Stanley Jevons.
The Logic of Statistics.

Prof. Michael Foster, M.D.
Protoplasm and the Cell Theory.

Rev. M. J. Berkeley, M.A., F.L.S.
Fungi: their Nature, Influences, and Uses.

Prof. Claude Bernard.
Physical and Metaphysical Phenomena of Life.

Prof. A. Quetelet.
Social Physics.

Prof. H. Sainte Claire Deville.
An Introduction to General Chemistry.

Prof. Wurtz.
Atoms and the Atomic Theory.

Prof. D. Quatrefages.
The Negro Races.

Prof. Lacaze-Duthiers.
Zoology since Cuvier.

Prof. Berthelot.
Chemical Synthesis.

Prof. J. Rosenthal.
(Subject not yet received.)

Prof. James D. Dana, M.A., LL.D.
On Cephalization; or, Head-Characters in the Gradation and Progress of Life.

Prof. S. W. Johnson, M.A.
On the Nutrition of Plants.

Prof. Austin Flint, Jr., M.D.
The Nervous System and its Relation to the Bodily Functions.

Prof. W. D. Whitney.
Modern Linguistic Science.

HENRY S. KING & CO.,
65, CORNHILL, AND 12, PATERNOSTER ROW, LONDON.

www.ingramcontent.com/pod-product-compliance
Lightning Source LLC
Chambersburg PA
CBHW022117230426
43672CB00008B/1413